Synkria™:

Seven Scientific Laws
That Shape Our Living Experience

Mithun Kamath

ISBN: *978-93-5635-880-5*

For those who never stopped asking why—
and for those who looked at life and thought,
there has to be more to this than meets the eye.

When we observe, life observes back—
and between the two, reality begins.

Contents

Introduction

A Crinkle in the Soul

Your body renews and destroys about 25 million cells every second. Each day, your senses process around 74 gigabytes of information—the equivalent of watching sixteen HD movies.

You are spinning at 1,000 miles per hour, orbiting the Sun at 67,000 miles per hour, and racing through the galaxy at over half a million miles per hour—all while feeling perfectly still. You live in a universe with about 300 sextillion planets *(if you haven't heard of "sextillion," it comes after billion, trillion, quadrillion, and quintillion)*—yet 95 percent of it remains unseen, made of dark matter and dark energy we still cannot explain.

For all this vastness and mystery, most of us live within a narrow view. Our brain, tuned to survive, processes reality through five limited senses and a three dimensional lens. We cannot see the ultraviolet patterns a bee follows on a flower, or smell the intricate world a dog perceives in a single sniff. We cannot sense the quiet hum of electromagnetic fields around us or feel the subtle gravitational pulls of distant planets. What we call "reality" is only what our instruments of perception allow us to see — a thin slice of a vast, interconnected whole.

Even as technology stretches our horizons—through telescopes that peer into galaxies, probes that touch the ocean floor, and machines that map the living brain—its revelations seldom change how we live. Most of us still move through life enclosed in a narrow circle of experience: what affects me today? What do I see, touch, taste, or hear?

Yet we are not apart from the universe we study. We are made of its dust, moved by its rhythms, bound by its laws. Some part of us knows this, even if dimly—and it is from here that our lifelong questions arise:

Why am I here? What explains sudden tragedy or luck? How can I be happy? Is life a set of accidents or destiny at play? Do I have a purpose, or is everything random?

For centuries, we have leaned on familiar explanations—luck, chance, fate, randomness, destiny. Each carries some truth, yet none feel complete. They leave behind a quiet ache, an unanswered hum beneath the surface of our understanding—*a crinkle in the soul.*

The Unseen Framework

When I began searching for answers to this quiet ache, I noticed something peculiar about how we humans seek understanding. We break the whole into parts and study them in isolation.

Physics explains motion, biology explains life, psychology explains mind, philosophy explains meaning. Each discipline builds its own walls, forgetting they all describe the same universe. But the universe itself knows no such boundaries. Gravity doesn't stop at the edge of chemistry. The laws that govern galaxies also shape the cells within us.

So I began to look not *within* a single field, but *across* them. I listened for the echoes that repeated through science, philosophy, and lived experience—the constants that seemed to hold everything together. Slowly, patterns emerged. They were not rules written by humans, but **currents** life has always followed—governing galaxies, rivers, societies, and thoughts alike.

What took shape was a set of seven fundamental truths.

I call them **Laws**, not as commandments, but as observations of how reality sustains itself. They shape the cosmos, and by extension, they shape us. Whether we acknowledge them or not, they move quietly through every choice, every outcome, every relationship—like gravity, waiting for no one's belief to operate

Here they are:

1. **The Law of the Observer Effect — Reality Begins When You Observe.**
   At the smallest scales, particles shift their behavior when watched. So too in life—what we choose to notice grows more real. Our attention doesn't just record reality; it helps create it.

2. **The Law of Uncertainty and Ambiguity — The Unknown Holds Creation.**
   The universe is not fixed but fluid—many possibilities exist until one unfolds. Ambiguity is not the enemy of clarity; it is the birthplace of all new forms and ideas.

3. **The Law of Entropy — Disorder Fuels Renewal.**
   Every system drifts toward chaos unless new energy enters. Decay, collapse, and confusion are not endings but openings for transformation. Change is life's way of staying alive.

4. **The Law of the Living Body — Our Bodies Know More Than We Do.**
   Each of us is a self-healing, sensing, adapting ecosystem—billions of cells collaborating in silent intelligence. Within this living system, wisdom moves without instruction.

5. **The Law of Equilibrium — Opposites Seek Balance.**
   Tension and resolution, rise and fall, gain and loss—each seeks its counterweight. Balance is not stillness but the movement that restores harmony across the universe and within us.

6. **The Law of Interconnectedness — Everything Shapes Everything Else.**
   Nothing stands alone. Every event, thought, and action is linked through invisible threads of cause and effect. What seems random is only what we cannot yet see in the web of connection.

7. **The Law of Evolution — Life Learns by Becoming.**
   Nothing in nature stays the same. Every challenge, mutation, or adaptation pushes life forward. Evolution is not just biology—it is the unfolding story of growth itself.

Each of these laws applies universally—to stars and rivers, to ecosystems and families, to cells and societies. More importantly, they do not act one at a time. They operate together, all at once, layering influence upon influence. This simultaneity is why life often feels complex, chaotic, or contradictory: seven laws working on us at once, intersecting and overlapping.

This book is about learning to see these laws—not as abstract theories, but as living forces shaping our everyday existence.

Enter Synkria™: The Art of Moving With Life

If these laws are always at play, the question is not whether we believe in them—they function regardless of belief. The real question is: *how do we live with them?*

Here is where I found an answer: **Synkria.**

From *Syn* (together) and *Kria* (action, in Sanskrit), *Synkria* means the union of observation, reflection, and mindful action. It is the art of moving in harmony with the laws that already govern our lives—neither resisting nor denying, but flowing with them.

To live Synkria is to say to life, "I see your motion, and I will move with it." It is the difference between fighting a river's current and learning to navigate with it. The current will always flow—my only choice is whether to exhaust myself in resistance, or to learn its patterns and let it carry me toward purpose.

What You'll Find in This Book

Each chapter unfolds through three movements:

- **Science** grounds each law in how the universe truly works.
- **Reflections** translate that knowledge into the language of daily life.
- **Synkria** Practices turn insight into simple, repeatable actions.

As you move through the chapters, these ideas will begin to converge—until, in the final section, we bring them all together. There, you'll discover how Renewal, Balance, and Connection become the living expression of everything you've read—the way to live Synkria each day. It is where understanding becomes embodiment.

By the end of this journey, you will not just know these laws—you will begin to *see* them moving through you and around you: in conversation, in conflict, in creation. Once seen, they can never be unseen.

And when that happens, life stops feeling random and begins to reveal its quiet design—one that has always included you.

A Different Lens

This book is not about debunking faith, magic, or destiny. It is about offering a different lens to understand our lived experience. Behind the mystery lies structure. Behind the apparent chaos lies coherence. Life is not a series of disconnected accidents, but a woven whole — a living fabric shaped by these seven laws moving together.

The question is not: *Do these laws exist?*

The question is: *Am I paying attention?*

Because once we begin to notice them, once we live in alignment with them, life stops feeling random and starts to reveal its quiet design. And in that design, we find not just explanation, but meaning. It did this for me. I hope it does for you.

Welcome to Synkria. Let's begin.

The Law of the Observer Effect

Reality is shaped by our observation

Full of excitement, she picked up her three tourists for a walking tour of the city she loved so much, wanting to immerse them in the energy, the colours and the life that made her city sing.

They wound their way through narrow lanes until the street opened into the plaza, alive with motion — the city's pulsing heart. Strings of coloured lights tangled overhead. Crowds milled about, busy in animated conversations. Vendors called out from food stalls, the air thick with the scent of roasting chestnuts and spiced bread. Laughter flared from a café terrace. Somewhere, a street musician coaxed a tune from a worn violin.

She let them soak it all in, surrounded by the same swirl of sound and colour. After a while, the guide asked with barely hidden pride, "How does this place make you feel?"

The first, eyes wide with wonder, spoke of laughter and movement — of the joy in people's faces, of children running between tables, the swirl of dresses and the way lights danced on the cobblestones.

The second frowned and exclaimed, "It's too loud. Too bright, too crowded. I can't think. I need to get out of here."

The third, smiling faintly, distracted and with eyes closed, said, "The food, the smells, the sizzle — I could stay here forever just tasting everything."

She looked at them, incredulous — three travellers standing in the same square, under the same lights, surrounded by the same sounds — yet seeing three completely different worlds.

As they walked on, she felt a quiet awe settle in — the world, she realised, doesn't exist as one thing waiting to be seen. It becomes what each of us observes.

The simple act of observing changes what is observed. This is not metaphor, but one of the strangest, most consistent findings across disciplines — physics, psychology, biology, sociology, even ecology. The observer is never outside the system; they are part of it. What we notice, what we attend to, and even what we expect reshapes reality itself.

Quantum Mechanics — Reality Waits to Be Seen

In the double-slit experiment, light and electrons behave like waves when unobserved, spreading as probabilities across a screen. Yet the instant they are measured, they collapse into particles — fixed points, as if they "decide" in response to being seen. Erwin Schrödinger captured this mystery in a thought experiment: a cat sealed in a box is both alive and dead until someone opens the lid.

Reality, at its smallest scales, refuses to commit until observed. Physicist John Wheeler called it a *participatory universe:* the cosmos awaits our glance to choose which possibility becomes real.

We are not so different. In our lives too, many possibilities exist at once — until we look at one closely enough to make it true.

Heisenberg's Microscope — To Look Is to Touch

Werner Heisenberg showed that to measure anything is to disturb it. Using a photon to observe an electron inevitably changes the electron's path. Observation requires interaction, and interaction means change.

The same is true of human encounters: to look deeply at another person is to alter them, and ourselves, in small invisible ways. Every act of attention is also an act of influence. To look, in any sense, is to touch.

The Body Observes Itself — Biology and Belief

The placebo effect reveals how expectation turns into biology. When a patient believes they are receiving medicine, the body begins to respond — releasing endorphins, easing pain, accelerating recovery — even if the pill is inert. Belief becomes chemical.

In biofeedback therapy, this self-observation becomes deliberate: by watching their own heart rate or muscle tension on a screen, patients learn to regulate it. Simply watching their own signals enables people to alter them—an observation that becomes a form of self-influence .

Our bodies, it seems, listen to what the mind observes. What we expect, we begin to experience.

Human Performance — We Become What Is Seen

In the 1920s, at the Hawthorne Works factory, researchers found that workers' productivity improved whenever they knew they were being studied — regardless of conditions. The *Hawthorne Effect* was born: awareness of being seen changes behavior.

In 1968, psychologist Robert Rosenthal gave teachers random lists of "gifted" children. The labels were false, yet by year's end those children outperformed their peers. Teachers' expectations changed how they treated them, which in turn changed the children's results. Expectation became reality.

To be seen as capable, valued, or loved often makes it so. Observation, in this sense, is participation in another's becoming.

Attention Creates Its Own Reality — What We Miss, We Create

In a now-famous experiment, researchers Daniel Simons and Christopher Chabris asked participants to count basketball passes. Half never noticed a person in a gorilla suit strolling across the scene. Magicians have known this for centuries—guiding attention to one hand while the other performs the trick. We see only what we attend to or shown; the rest quietly falls away.

At the same time, we overestimate how much others notice about us — a phenomenon called the *spotlight effect.* We imagine ourselves perpetually watched, our small errors magnified. Children form self-concepts through caregiver feedback; adults absorb subtle cues from colleagues, strangers, and society. Experiments in "social mirroring" show how even facial expressions from others alter moods and behaviors. But the truth is gentler: others are too absorbed in their own fields of attention.

Attention both reveals and conceals. It is a lens that clarifies one world and erases another. And to be observed is not neutral—it is formative. What we fail to see is not gone — only waiting for us to look.

The Gaze of Others — Identity in Observation

Human beings are social mirrors. From infancy, we learn who we are through the eyes of others — first caregivers, then friends, strangers, and societies. To be seen with kindness strengthens us; to be misjudged distorts our sense of self.

Even our digital lives echo this: social media algorithms are built on observation. They feed us more of what we look at, shaping our moods and beliefs, and in turn, we shape our posts for being seen, translated into comments, reactions and likes. In our times, the knowledge of what people observe has become one of the most powerful forces of control, persuasion, and influence

We are continuously negotiating between being the observer and the observed — each reflection refining or refracting who we believe ourselves to be.

Neuroplasticity — The Brain as a Mirror

Neuroscience shows that the brain changes in response to what it repeatedly observes. Focused attention — whether playing the piano, learning a language, or practicing mindfulness — strengthens neural pathways. MRI scans reveal that even imagining movement can rewire motor regions of the brain.

Where attention goes, neurons grow. Each moment of focused observation sculpts the organ through which we observe. Our minds are not only witnesses to life; they are shaped by what they choose to notice.

From the quantum to the social, the lesson repeats: to observe is to alter. Each act of attention collapses possibilities into one unfolding reality. The question, then, is no longer *whether* we shape the world, but *how* we do it — with fear, with curiosity, or with care. What we notice becomes our world. What we ignore, vanishes from it. Reality waits, always, for the direction of our gaze.

Realizing the power of observation lead me to an obvious question: *Am I observing in ways that create the best possible reality for me?* When I explored this question, some surprising realizations emerged.

Synkria Reflections: What the Observer Effect Means in My Life

The Lenses I Didn't Choose

From childhood, society handed me lenses through which to see the world—grades, wealth, titles, possessions. They became success filters shaping how I measured myself and others. The rich and famous became my silent role models, and possessions quietly stood in for self-worth.

Over time, I saw what these lenses were doing. They made my world smaller - a narrow, distorted reality, stripped of the richness around me. I missed the quiet, immeasurable things that make life whole—kindness, patience, curiosity, humility & sacrifice.

To change my world, I had to change my lens. Honest observation—of my strengths, limitations, and desires—creates a truer reality than society's borrowed definitions ever could.

The Lenses I Use Shape Others Too

The same filters that shape how I see myself distort how I see others. When I rank people by power, wealth, or status, I see fragments, not people.

When I set those lenses aside, I began to see whole people. I saw quiet healers who give without recognition, loving parents sacrificing without expectations, determined entrepreneurs creating livelihoods, teachers whose wisdom carries whole generations, courageous activities making our world a better place. I began to see the flaws in my heroes and the extraordinary in everyone else.

Psychology calls this the Rosenthal effect: what I expect, I help to bring forth. If I observe only flaws, people shrink under my gaze. If I observe strengths, people grow. My observation is not neutral—it calls one version of them into being.

Observation Creates the Reality I Live In

Consider Erik Weihenmayer, who lost his sight at thirteen but chose to observe ability rather than disability. He became the first blind person to summit Mount Everest, then climbed the Seven Summits and kayaked the

Grand Canyon. His story isn't about ignoring limitation but about choosing what to observe.

That choice exists for me too. This very book is a result of what I chose to notice—my capacity to reflect, to connect ideas, to create meaning. Many versions of me were possible; I made this one real by observing it into being.

Observation, guided by curiosity instead of judgment, can uncover entire lives within us we never knew existed.

Seeing Only Half Distorts the Whole

For years, I lived inside the old metaphor of the glass—half full or half empty. But the truth is simpler and stranger: the glass is both. The error lies in observing only half.

Attentional blindness shows this in the lab: we miss the gorilla in the room while counting basketball passes. In life, we do the same—seeing only what we prefer, missing what challenges us. Optimists and pessimists alike are trapped by selective vision.

Balance requires not judgment but courage—the courage to look at the whole glass, even when one side is hard to see.

Wonder Lives in How I Look, Not What I See

The mind loves patterns. We seek repetition to feel safe, yet the same patterns can dull wonder. Every sunrise seems identical, every daily ritual predictable—until I look closer. No dawn repeats itself; clouds, light, and air never align the same way twice.

I once thought compatibility in relationships was about sameness—shared tastes, shared views, shared routines. But over time, I noticed relationships rise or collapse not on sameness but on what each person chose to observe. If I observe only differences, conflict grows. If I observe only commonalities, I ignore the real work of navigating difference. Healthy relationships require the full gaze: to see both tensions and harmonies, and to hold them together without denial.

The same applies to work, play or art. What grows stale is not the world, but my gaze upon it. Repetition without renewed observation numbs me; change what I notice, and everything comes alive again.

A zebra's stripes, a sunset's hue, the cadence of a friend's voice—each unique once I care enough to look. Wonder, I have learned, is not in what I see, but in how I see.

Observation Guided by Impact Reveals Purpose

Purpose isn't something hidden in the distance—it's what appears when I observe the impact of my actions. When I truly see what my choices set in motion, meaning crystallizes.

A simple act like brushing my teeth connects me to farmers who grew the ingredients, to factories that shaped the brush, to the ecosystems that carry away its waste. A car salesman, thinking he merely sells vehicles, is really shaping families' commutes, memories, and journeys.

Observation guided by impact collapses meaning into being. It shows me that even my smallest actions are nodes in a vast, living network. Purpose hides in the ordinary, waiting for me to see it.

Observation Is Mindfulness Itself

I once thought mindfulness was a discipline, something to "practice." Now I see it for what it is: pure observation. When I notice how I breathe, how I walk, how I speak, life slows into presence. Attention refines action; awareness transforms it.

Every small noticing—each breath, glance, or heartbeat—is life becoming conscious of itself. The more I observe, the more I participate in creating the world that observes me back.

Synkria Practises: What Can I Do With the Observer Effect?

If observation shapes reality, then Synkria asks me to use my gaze with care. I cannot stop observing — every moment, my attention lands somewhere. But I can choose *what* and *how* I observe. These small shifts change what becomes real.

See Potential, Not Chaos

The world can easily look like disorder — with affirmation from a storm of headlines, comparisons, and noise. Yet, new discoveries, exploration and progress are taking place every day. Reflection, the very heart of Synkria, helps me decide what deserves my attention and what does not.

When I choose to see potential instead of confusion, I begin to notice quiet opportunities where I once saw clutter. The moment I change my observation, the world changes dramatically. The world is both chaos and creation – my observation decides which becomes real.

See People as Whole

Observation shapes not just my world, but the people in it. To "see the good" is easy; to see people completely — strengths, flaws, contradictions together — is harder.

Everyone carries all three. When I observe others this way, something changes: judgment softens, forgiveness becomes possible, and connection deepens. It helps me forgive, draw on others' strengths, and normalize relationships so they grow stronger. Wholeness in others restores wholeness in me.

Internal Growth is What You Observe

Neuroplasticity shows that neurons grow where attention goes. When I observe harmony, my body learns calm; when I notice creativity, ideas arrive; when I observe joy, I begin to smile.

Attention is not neutral — it is an investment. Through practices like journaling, gratitude, and mindful reflection, I can direct my gaze toward qualities I wish to cultivate. I am limited only by the boundaries of my own observation.

Refresh Your Gaze

Habit narrows vision. Commutes, conversations, routines become invisible through repetition. Yet every ordinary act hides a thousand unseen details — a change in the light, the face of a stranger, the quiet rhythm of life.

To keep life vivid, I must keep changing what I observe. When I renew my attention, the mundane regains its magic. Wonder returns not because the world has changed, but because I changed the way I see.

Synkria – Try Me

The observer effect requires both discipline and practice: discipline to quiet the noise of the mind, and practice to choose what we truly want to observe. The first begins with attention to the ordinary; the second, with attention to the mind itself.

Practice One: Observation Changes the Act

Choose one ordinary activity you do every day — a walk, brushing your teeth, making tea, commuting to work. Look for details you normally miss. Notice your feelings as you make new or unseen observations. You may find that the act itself begins to change, responding to your gaze.

Practice Two: Train Your Neurons Where to Grow

Catch one negative loop in your mind — self-criticism, fear, judgment — or one block that keeps you from trying something new: learning an instrument, taking a solo trip, speaking up in a meeting.

Redirect your attention toward one strength, one possibility, one moment of courage, or one reason to try. Notice how your feelings shift as you observe differently — each time you redirect your attention, you sculpt your inner reality.

The Law of Uncertainty & Ambiguity

Uncertainty, ambiguity, and probability lie at the heart of existence.

It was early morning when she reached the old suspension bridge. A soft fog had rolled in overnight, swallowing the river and the path beyond. From where she stood, only the first few planks were visible — the rest dissolved into white. She hesitated. Crossing meant stepping into what she could not see.

For a long while, she waited for the mist to lift, hoping the path would reveal itself. But it didn't. The world stayed quiet, suspended between form and formlessness. Finally, she took a breath and stepped forward. Each plank appeared only when her foot touched it, and the bridge — invisible moments before — kept building itself beneath her weight.

When she reached the other side, the fog was still there, unchanged. What had changed was her — she now knew that not everything must be visible to be trusted.

We spend much of life waiting for the fog to lift — for clarity before we act, for certainty before we choose. Yet, like the bridge that revealed itself only when stepped upon, reality often discloses itself through movement, not before it. The universe, it turns out, operates by the same law. Beneath everything we see is a world built on uncertainty — particles that exist as probabilities, patterns that defy prediction, systems that thrive on change. Ambiguity is not an accident in nature; it is its very architecture. Science, too, has begun to uncover this truth — that uncertainty is not a flaw in the design of the universe, but its foundation.

Heisenberg's Uncertainty Principle – The Limits of Knowing

In the smallest theatres of existence, the universe resists being pinned down. When scientists tried to measure the position of an electron with greater accuracy, its motion blurred. When they tried to capture its speed, its location vanished into probability. This is not because our instruments are inadequate, but because nature itself refuses total disclosure.

Werner Heisenberg's Uncertainty Principle revealed that at quantum scales, *to know one thing completely is to lose sight of another.* Every measurement changes what is being measured. Reality, at its foundation, is not a fixed arrangement of objects but a field of possibilities. The deeper we look, the more the edges dissolve. What we call the *unknown* may simply be the space where the universe keeps its freedom to move.

At our scale too, life behaves much the same way. The moment we try to define it too tightly — a relationship, a plan, even our sense of self — it begins to shift. The more we try to control outcomes, the more unpredictable they become. Heisenberg's discovery whispers a simple truth: certainty is not the nature of reality but a comfort of the mind. Existence is not meant to be pinned down; it is meant to be participated in.

Wave–Particle Duality – The Nature of the In-Between

Light, one of the most familiar things in our world, holds a secret. When passed through a narrow slit, it spreads out like a wave. But when the same experiment is observed particle by particle, it behaves as though it were made of tiny bullets. How can something be both continuous and discrete, both fluid and solid?

This puzzle — known as wave–particle duality — lies at the heart of quantum physics. The behavior of light and matter depends on how they are observed. Under one condition, they travel as waves; under another, they appear as particles. They are not switching forms, but revealing different aspects of the same underlying reality.

In a sense, the universe itself refuses to pick a side. It doesn't declare, "I am this, not that." It holds both possibilities at once, waiting for context to call one forward. And in that, it mirrors life: we too contain contradictions

— rational yet emotional, certain yet unsure. Our nature, like light, is not singular but fluid, capable of many expressions depending on how we are seen and how we see ourselves.

Chaos Theory – Predictability Has Edges

We often imagine that if we just knew enough, we could predict everything. Yet nature works differently. In the 1960s, meteorologist Edward Lorenz discovered that a minuscule change in a weather model — something as tiny as rounding a number from 0.506127 to 0.506 — produced a completely different forecast. This sensitivity became known as the *Butterfly Effect* — the idea that the flap of a butterfly's wings in Brazil could, in theory, set off a tornado in Texas.

This is **chaos theory:** systems governed by clear rules can still behave unpredictably. Weather patterns, ocean currents, heart rhythms, even the rise and fall of populations — all follow laws of motion, yet their future states cannot be precisely known. Small variations amplify until the outcome escapes foresight.

The same holds true for us. We cannot predict our own futures, even when we perform the seemingly right actions with perfect intent. A single shift in one of the countless variables that shape our lives — a conversation, a delay, a change in mood — can alter everything. And because we live in an interconnected universe, we can never know all the forces at play. Our efforts to create order — every plan, every decision — are carried out within a field of larger, unknowable chaos. That is why prediction, however careful, will always remain an act of faith.

Evolution and Mutation – Nature's Risk Engine

Every living thing on Earth exists because nature is willing to take risks. When cells divide, they copy their DNA — billions of chemical letters that hold the code for life. But sometimes, an error slips in: a single letter misplaced, a sequence repeated or deleted. Most of these mistakes change nothing. Some cause harm. And a rare few open the door to something new — a trait that helps an organism survive better in its environment.

This is evolution's hidden genius: progress born from uncertainty. Mutation is not a failure in the system; it *is* the system. Life evolves not through perfect replication but through a delicate balance of order and error — trial, feedback, and adaptation over time.

In our own lives, the same law quietly operates. We often treat mistakes as disruptions, but they are the raw material of learning and growth. Every misstep alters our trajectory, sometimes in ways that only make sense much later. Nature doesn't avoid uncertainty; it uses it to move forward.

The Biology of Uncertainty – The Body's Alarm

The human body is wired to seek predictability. For most of our evolutionary history, uncertainty meant danger — an unfamiliar sound in the dark, a rustle in the grass, a change in the wind. Our nervous system evolved to respond instantly: the **amygdala** fired, signaling threat; **adrenaline** surged; the heart raced; **cortisol** primed the body for action. This was the *fight-or-flight* response — nature's way of keeping us alive in a world that changed without warning.

But in modern life, the same ancient circuitry is triggered by far gentler uncertainties — a delayed message, an ambiguous tone, an uncertain future. The body reacts to them as if they were predators, flooding our system with stress hormones that prepare us to run, though there's nowhere to go. Our biology, built for survival, struggles to distinguish between physical threat and psychological uncertainty.

In the wild, animals have mastered this balance. A herd of deer grazing on a plain remains alert to every sound — ears twitching, eyes scanning. A rustle in the wind makes them attentive, but they do not flee. Only when the predator reveals itself does the chase begin. And when the danger passes, something remarkable happens: within moments, they return to feeding, as though the near-death pursuit never occurred. Their bodies know how to complete the stress cycle — to move from tension back to calm. Humans, by contrast, often stay trapped in the chase long after it has ended, replaying the threat in our minds. The body is safe, but the mind keeps running. We need to relearn from animals what neuroscience calls *rapid stress recovery* — the ability to activate and deactivate the stress response quickly and completely.

The Brain and Ambiguity – From Threat to Curiosity

The human brain is a prediction machine. It constantly compares what it expects with what it perceives, updating its map of reality moment by moment. This predictive rhythm keeps us safe — it helps us recognize patterns, anticipate consequences, and move through the world with confidence. But when something unpredictable happens, that internal map falters. The mind enters a gap between what it knows and what it cannot yet explain. That gap is ambiguity.

In that instant, two ancient forces awaken. The **amygdala** sounds the alarm, treating uncertainty as potential threat. The body tenses, the pulse quickens, thought narrows to survival. But alongside this circuitry, another system comes online: the **prefrontal cortex** and **anterior cingulate cortex,** regions that enable curiosity, problem-solving, and flexible thinking. Which path we follow — fear or curiosity — determines how we experience uncertainty.

Psychology calls this *ambiguity tolerance* — the ability to stay open when the outcome is unclear. People with higher tolerance for ambiguity tend to be more creative, adaptable, and emotionally resilient. They don't rush to close the gap between question and answer; they explore it. When we learn to hold uncertainty without panic, the same neural energy that once fuelled anxiety begins to power imagination. In this way, ambiguity becomes not a flaw in the design of the mind, but its most fertile condition for growth.

Creativity – Using Uncertainty to Power the Body and Mind

When we create — when we dance, sing, paint, or write — we are not merely expressing ourselves; we are entering a biological state of uncertainty. The brain loosens its grip on prediction and control, allowing new patterns to emerge.

Neuroscientists studying artists and athletes have found that during deep creative immersion, a phenomenon called *transient hypofrontality* occurs — the **prefrontal cortex,** which manages self-monitoring, time perception, and judgment, temporarily quiets down. This allows the rest of the brain to operate more freely, unrestrained by self-critique or rigid logic. When that happens, we lose track of time and self. Psychologist **Mihaly Csikszentmihalyi** called this state *flow* — what we often describe as being "in the zone." Paradoxically, creativity thrives when the very parts of the brain responsible for control momentarily let go.

Creativity also activates the brain's **dopamine pathways** — particularly in the *nucleus accumbens* and *ventral tegmental area.* These regions light up not only when we succeed but when we *anticipate* discovery. This means creativity is literally rewarding. We are wired to enjoy exploration — the thrill of "what if?"

Neuroscience shows that creativity arises from a **collaboration of opposites** — between the *Default Mode Network* (the seat of imagination and memory) and the *Executive Control Network* (responsible for focus and discipline). In ordinary life, these networks alternate. But in moments of creation, they synchronize. Dreams and logic, intuition and structure, ambiguity and clarity — they begin to converse. The result is a neurological duet between freedom and form.

Movement, rhythm, and sound activate the **motor cortex, cerebellum,** and **limbic system,** harmonizing motion with emotion. Singing, chanting, and deep breathing stimulate the **vagus nerve,** calming the autonomic nervous system. The body enters coherence — heart rate, breath, and brain waves align — producing a measurable reduction in stress and an increase in emotional stability. The very act of creating becomes a biological repair — a way the body learns that uncertainty can be not only safe, but life-giving.

Synkria Reflections: Living with Uncertainty

Uncertainty Is the Order

Uncertainty rises in me from the mind's need to know — from my endless search for order while living in a vast, shifting web of chaos. This conflict is inevitable: seeking permanence in constant motion makes uncertainty not an exception, but a guarantee.

Most of us react to this by tightening up — trying to manage the unmanageable. Our biology leaps into fight or flight, our thoughts race to predict, our emotions swing between worry and control. It shows up in everyday phrases — *"I'm taking it one day at a time",* or the sigh behind a simple *"I'm managing."* Beneath them all lies a quiet confession: *I don't know what comes next.*

But something changes when I stop seeing uncertainty as a flaw in the system and start seeing it as the system itself. Order, when seen as uncertainty, changes the game. Life is not a single road but a series of forks — each one asking me to pause, sense, and choose. Every fork is possibility in disguise.

When I treat uncertainty as the natural order of things, my mind reorganizes itself. Anxiety gives way to alertness, and fear turns into curiosity.

I begin to live with energy and coherence — not because I know what will happen, but because I am part of what is happening.

So when life asks me, *"How are you?"*, my truest answer is no longer *"I'm managing."*

It is, *"I'm exploring."*

Chaos Requires Constant Engagement

Chaos unsettles me because it keeps moving. Nothing stays the same long enough to hold on to. At first, this feels disorienting — like standing on shifting sand. But once I move past the discomfort, the answer becomes clear: in a world that never stops changing, I too must keep moving. Exploration and constant engagement are not choices; they are necessities.

When I stay engaged — thinking, creating, reflecting, acting — I feel connected to life again. My energy finds direction. The more I engage, the less powerless I feel. Chaos doesn't shrink, but I grow larger within it.

Constant engagement is not restlessness; it is rhythm. Some days it takes the form of work, some days of rest, but always of participation. When I stop engaging, anxiety returns — not because the world changed, but because I stopped moving with it.

Chaos will always exist. But when I keep saying to myself, *"I'm at it,"* I realize I'm not waiting for the bridge to appear — I'm already taking the next step on it.

Variety Is the Spice That Cures Uncertainty

Routine gives me comfort, but too much of it narrows my life. When I keep repeating the same patterns, I build a small world — predictable, safe, and quietly suffocating. Even a small disruption — a delayed flight, a change at work, a sudden illness — can then feel like collapse. I've learned that uncertainty hurts most when life is built on too little variety.

Grandma's advice — *"have a hobby"* — was more than simple wisdom; it was biology in disguise. Variety exercises different parts of my brain and body. When I paint, walk, cook, or listen to music, each act wakes up a new circuit, releases new energy, and refreshes the tired grooves of habit. Doing many things isn't distraction; it's balance.

I used to think discipline meant doing the same thing every day. Now I see that true discipline is doing many things fully — work, rest, movement, stillness, solitude, connection. Variety keeps my mind fluid, my body adaptable, and my spirit light.

When life changes suddenly, I no longer freeze. I shift. Because variety has trained me to live with change, not fear it.

The Inverse Proportion Between Knowing Myself and Uncertainty

The more I try to define who I am, the smaller my world becomes. Each label — capable, incapable, creative, practical — fixes me in place. And the more fixed I become, the more uncertain life feels. I start fearing what doesn't fit my definition.

Physics tells me that a particle exists in many possible states until it is observed. Perhaps I'm not so different. Every time I say, *"I can't,"* I collapse my own possibilities. But when I say, *"Let me try,"* I open a new pathway for discovery.

The most alive moments of my life have come not from certainty but from exploration — when I stepped into something I didn't yet know how to do. Each time I said yes to an experience that scared or stretched me, I became a little larger.

As I age, I see how easy it is to shrink — to stay within routines, opinions, and familiar skills. But when I keep saying yes, uncertainty stops feeling like a threat. It becomes a mirror reflecting everything I can still become.

I don't need to know myself fully. I just need to keep discovering who I am.

Creativity Is Not an Event, It's a Way of Life

I used to think creativity belonged to a chosen few — artists, writers, inventors. But I've come to see that creativity isn't about what we do; it's about how we move through the unknown. Every moment invites me to respond in a new way, to make something out of what wasn't there before — an idea, a solution, a way forward.

When I cook without a recipe, speak from the heart, or find a new path through an old problem, I am creating. Each act, however small, asks me to trust uncertainty — to let something emerge before I can name it. Creativity isn't a skill; it's a relationship with the unknown.

This way of living turns the ordinary into a canvas. The day stops being a list of tasks and becomes a series of possibilities. When I meet life this way — alert, curious, willing — even washing dishes becomes an act of discovery.

Creativity, I've realized, is not an event that happens to me. It is the way I meet everything that happens.

Synkria Practises – Living With Uncertainty as the Order

Living with uncertainty is perhaps the hardest of all Synkria practices. It goes against my oldest wiring — the instincts of a creature built to predict danger and seek control. For thousands of years, this reflex has kept me safe. But in today's world, it often works against me. My mind treats every unknown as a threat; it resists ambiguity the way the body resists pain.

I've learned that trying to think my way out of uncertainty rarely works. The mind may understand, but the body still holds its alarms. The real shift comes not from ideas but from practice — from behaviours that teach my body to feel safe amid change. Over time, these behaviours become habits, and habits quietly rewire my responses.

I've found two that make the biggest difference. They are simple, fun, and almost immediate in effect. They help me move from tightness to flow, from fear to curiosity, and they remind me that uncertainty is not a problem to solve but the natural rhythm of life.

Introduce Variety in the Everyday — Without a Target

I used to move through my days like they were checklists. Work, eat, sleep, repeat — each action measured by some goal or outcome. But life feels different when I bring in small doses of variety — not to achieve anything, but just to experience.

Reading, walking, gardening, playing music, cooking something new, talking to a friend — these aren't distractions; they're cross-training for the mind. Each act wakes up a different network in the brain and gives it a small, healthy shock of novelty. Dopamine rises, attention shifts, and suddenly the day feels more alive.

The key is to do these things for no reason. Not to master them, not to be productive, but to play. When I let myself do something simply because it feels good, I teach my brain that uncertainty is safe. The more variety I live with, the more flexible I become — ready for whatever form the day takes.

Pursue One Creative Activity to Fire the Imagination

Of all the ways to live with uncertainty, creativity is the most natural teacher. When I paint, write, sing, or sculpt, I step into a space where I don't know what will happen next. Each stroke, each note, is a choice without guarantee — and yet it feels alive.

The creative act invites both imagination and emotion. It lets me express what I cannot explain. It also trains my mind to tolerate ambiguity — to stay with the unfinished, the imperfect, the unfolding. I've learned that it doesn't matter what form creativity takes; what matters is that it moves me. Ten minutes of it a day can change my state more than hours of analysis.

Our culture calls hobbies "good to have." But my body knows better — they are not luxuries, they are necessities. Creativity restores balance to my nervous system. It turns uncertainty from threat to possibility.

Like crossing a foggy bridge, the path ahead appears only as I take the next step. These practices don't promise clarity; they build trust in movement.

And that, I've realised, is the essence of living with uncertainty — to keep stepping, even when I cannot see the other side.

Synkria Try Me – Meeting the Unknown, Now

These aren't routines to maintain; they are brief encounters with the unknown — things you can do within the next hour to feel uncertainty shift from tension to curiosity. Each one is a doorway to lightness.

The Unplanned Choice

Right now, look around you and pick one small thing you can do differently — open a random page in a book, choose a song you've never heard, take a turn you don't usually take. Don't overthink it; just let curiosity choose for you.

Notice how your mind protests for control, then softens as surprise takes over. This is uncertainty in its mildest, most beautiful form — the unknown revealing itself as freshness.

The One-Line Creation

Take a piece of paper or your phone notes and write, draw, or hum *one spontaneous line.* Don't edit. Don't plan. It could be a sentence, a sketch, or a sound — anything that didn't exist a minute ago.

You've just created something from nothing. That's the purest act of living with uncertainty — watching clarity form out of openness.

The Micro-Exchange

Speak to someone you don't usually talk to — a neighbour, a colleague, a vendor — and ask one genuine question. It doesn't matter what about.

Every conversation with a stranger is a small act of courage. It reminds the nervous system that stepping into the unknown often brings connection, not danger.

Each of these takes minutes, yet shifts how I relate to uncertainty — from a thing to fix, to a field to explore. When I let small unpredictability's enter my day, life stops feeling like something to manage. It becomes something to meet.

The Law of Entropy

Everything drifts toward disorder unless energy is continuously invested to maintain structure.

A photograph rests on a wooden shelf, sunlight touching it each morning through a half-drawn curtain.

It once held crisp outlines — a face you loved, a landscape that spoke of another time. Now, its edges curl. The colors pale. Dust gathers on its frame. No one caused it. No hand tore it. It is simply time doing what time always does — turning order back into dust, light back into air.

One day, you pick it up and really look. The image stirs a quiet rush of memory — warmth, longing, love. For that moment, the past and the present, observer and observed, are woven together again.

With care, you wipe the dust away, carry it to be restored, and place it back on the same shelf.

And then, as always, time resumes its patient work.

The photograph is not alone in its fate. Everything that exists — from stars to stones to human memories, from the cooling of a cup of coffee to the fading of ink, from the decay of matter to the erosion of thought and habit — follows the same quiet law. This is the law of entropy: the universe's gentle but unwavering tilt toward disorder, the natural drift of all systems left unattended.

Yet even here, balance endures. The law of equilibrium ensures that entropy is not the end of order but its partner — that decay is continually met by renewal and transformation. And this renewal and transformation arise through interconnectedness — through the constant exchange of energy and influence between things.

This dance of natural entropy, balanced by renewal and transformation through interconnectedness, is woven through everything we know. Consider this:

The Second Law of Thermodynamics – The Arrow of Time

Heat will always move toward something colder. This is the Second Law of Thermodynamics — the law that gives the universe its forward momentum.

When energy disperses, it moves from concentrated to diffused — from useful to spent. A hot cup of tea cools as its warmth escapes into the room. The tea doesn't heat itself again, because that would require a spontaneous gathering of all its scattered heat energy — something nature never does on its own. To reverse that drift, energy must be added once more — by reheating, in this case.

This one-way movement of entropy — from concentrated to dispersed — is what we experience as the flow of time. Heat spreads and scatters; the direction of heat is the direction of time — always forward. Our sense of past, present, and future arises from this very flow: the past as the memory of the hot tea, the present as knowing it is cooling, the future as the thought of drinking it.

And since time moves only forward, we can make a memory but never unform it. What has been felt or known cannot be undone. Time, as we live it, is entropy in motion.

Stellar Life Cycles – Creation from Collapse

Stars shine because they are spending their stored energy. Inside their cores, hydrogen atoms fuse into helium, releasing heat and light. Over time, this fuel runs out. The balance between outward radiation and inward gravity falters, and the star begins to collapse.

A smaller star may quietly fade into a dense white dwarf; a larger one may end in a spectacular explosion called a supernova. In either case, heat, light, and matter spread outward into the universe. This debris from a dying star interacts with gravity, becoming the raw material for new stars and planets.

Luckily for us, one such planet — Earth — formed in perfect balance, allowing life to emerge. Everything within us, from the iron in our blood to the calcium in our bones, is born of this cosmic scattering. Entropy leads to collapse, while equilibrium and interconnectedness create renewal — a cycle of creation from collapse. The same law that cools a cup of tea now burns in the heart of our Sun and flows quietly in our blood.

Photosynthesis – Entropy and Interconnectedness

The universe sustains itself through a constant exchange — entropy in one place creating renewal in another. The Sun's heat and light, born from nuclear entropy, travel through space and touch the green surface of a leaf. There, energy that would otherwise fade into cold emptiness is caught and converted. Through photosynthesis, plants combine sunlight, water, and carbon dioxide to create food — fuel for all life.

Entropy starts this entire process. The Sun loses energy as it radiates light, but that loss becomes nourishment elsewhere. Interconnectedness turns decay into sustenance. A dying star gives warmth to a living planet; that warmth feeds a leaf; that leaf, in turn, feeds us.

For the plant, life is an oscillation between creating food and becoming food — between storing energy and returning it. The steamed vegetables on our dinner plate are a direct result of this rhythm between entropy and interconnectedness — the Sun's fading energy briefly held in form, before it too is released back into the cycle.

Cellular Renewal – Continuity Through Change

Every moment, life within us unravels and rebuilds itself. Billions of cells die, and billions more are born. The skin we touch, the blood that flows, the lining of our gut, our hair and nails — all are constantly replaced. You are never the same person twice, yet always recognizably yourself.

Our bodies are designed to work with entropy. Dead cells are recycled; their components repurposed to form new structures. Yet as time goes by, entropy ensures that this process slows — repair falters, renewal weakens, and the body eventually reaches its end. Death is the culmination of entropy within us.

And yet, continuity persists. We live on through our children, passing forward our chromosomes, DNA, and even the mitochondria inherited through maternal lineage. The act of creating new life itself is an expression of interconnectedness — an exchange of cells and coded memory.

Our bodies are living reminders of entropy, equilibrium, and interconnectedness working together. We owe our very existence to this delicate rhythm that has played out over millennia — the endless cycle of breakdown and renewal that sustains life.

Forest Ecosystems – The Wisdom of Rot

A forest floor is a laboratory of entropy. Fallen leaves, branches, and trees decompose slowly, breaking down into simpler forms. Fungi, bacteria, and insects feed on this decay, releasing nutrients back into the soil. Hyphae — the thin threads of fungi that connect to tree roots — form vast mycorrhizal networks, helping trees absorb these nutrients in exchange for sugars.

The forest doesn't fear decay. It understands it as the price of renewal. Every fallen leaf is the beginning of another spring. The forest uses entropy and interconnectedness to nourish its life.

Human life mirrors this wisdom. With age and experience, we outgrow old identities, relationships, and beliefs, making space for renewal. Our goals evolve, our priorities shift, and loss often becomes the ground from which new growth begins.

Entropy is inevitable, but in an interconnected universe, it is the beginning of renewal. Loss is not to be feared, but seen as the beginning of new things.

Ocean Currents and Climate – Balance Through Motion

The Earth maintains its balance through movement. Warm water from the equator flows toward the poles, while cold water sinks and travels back toward the tropics. These vast ocean currents act like the planet's circulation system — redistributing heat, nutrients, and energy. Without this constant motion, the world would fall into extremes: some regions unbearably hot, others frozen and lifeless.

Entropy sets this flow in motion. Heat always moves from warmer to cooler places, seeking balance. The oceans simply express this law on a planetary scale. Interconnected with the winds above and the continents they touch, they form a global system where every temperature shift and current ripple affects another.

Human life, too, depends on such movement. When we stagnate — in thought, routine, or feeling — entropy sets in and balance is lost. Renewal comes through motion: learning something new, changing our environment, or opening ourselves to new currents of experience. Just as the oceans have learned to live through movement, so must we — to flow, to learn, and to stay open.

Cognitive Entropy – The Mind's Need for Meaning

The mind, like any other system, moves toward disorder when left unattended. Thoughts scatter, attention drifts, and uncertainty takes over. This mental disarray is what psychologists call *cognitive entropy* — the tendency of the minyed to lose structure when it stops processing or integrating information coherently. Therefore, many people experience anxiety when there is nothing to process or integrate, and life begins to feel meaningless.

Our search for meaning is often about our *internal* experience of events, not the events themselves. The mind constantly seeks order. We shape our inner world through patterns and stories — giving emotion a place to rest, memory a direction, and thought a sense of balance. With love, the routine job of parenting becomes deeply meaningful. The loss of a loved one becomes bearable through remembrance and gratitude.

Interconnectedness also plays its role here. Our minds do not regulate in isolation. Conversation, reflection, and shared understanding restore structure where confusion once spread. Every time we talk, write, or listen, we exchange mental energy that helps reorder thought. That's why parenting groups exist, and why grief is shared.

When we stop engaging, the mind, like stagnant water, begins to cloud. Renewal requires movement — curiosity, dialogue, learning, and expression. Meaning-making is our psychological form of photosynthesis: transforming scattered thought into livable experience.

Social Systems – Renewal Through Decay

Human societies, like every living system, follow the law of entropy. Over time, structures lose efficiency, institutions become rigid, and ideas that once inspired begin to decay. Energy disperses — in the form of lost trust, outdated norms, or depleted innovation. Left unattended, every civilization tends toward disorder. History is proof: mighty empires, ancient religions, and entire systems of governance have vanished with time.

In human systems, entropy often moves at breakneck speed. Innovation and technology, while propelling progress, also accelerate change — constantly unsettling what once seemed stable. The result is a world in continual upheaval, where structures evolve faster than our ability to adapt. Yet, this is not new. A thousand years ago, people felt the same tremors of change. Entropy has always been at work.

When systems reach their limits, they make space for transformation — new ideas, new leadership, new ways of being. Reform, collaboration, and shared purpose re-channel dispersed energy into new forms of order. The civil rights movement reshaped morality; the birth of democracy redefined power; the digital revolution reimagined connection. Each emerged from breakdown — entropy giving rise to renewal.

Such transformation, however, is rarely systemic. It is brought forth by individuals who notice imbalance and reintroduce energy through empathy, innovation, and courage. Societies depend on people like you and me to renew them. Each of us holds the potential to restore balance — if we notice entropy and choose to act.

Synkria Reflections: What Entropy means in my life

Entropy is happening all around us — in stars burning out, forests renewing themselves, oceans circulating warmth, and minds seeking meaning. I realized that the same law moves quietly within me — in my body, my relationships, my work, and my thoughts.

To understand entropy is to recognize that I am not separate from it. I live inside its current — sometimes carried by it, sometimes pushing against it, always shaped by its flow. As I turned my gaze inward to see how this plays out in daily life, I began to understand how to experience entropy — and how to balance it through renewal, awareness, and connection. These reflections grew from that realization.

I Am Both Facing Entropy and Its Counterbalance

If entropy is happening all around me, then I am not separate from it — I am within it. My body, my thoughts, my relationships, even my routines are constantly shifting toward disorder. Yet, within the same moment, I hold the power to renew, to realign, to bring energy back into form. I am both the falling leaf and the hand that clears it.

This realization is deeply humbling and profoundly empowering. It means that every choice I make — to learn, to care, to repair, to begin again — tilts the balance, however slightly, toward renewal. My smallest acts ripple through the web around me, changing its shape in ways I may never see.

I am not outside the universe observing entropy; I am its participant and its counterforce. Every breath I take, every word I speak, every act of attention I give is part of this eternal exchange. I am the system in motion, and the energy that sustains it.

From Seeing Snapshots to Understanding Motion

Entropy taught me to change how I see the world. Everything around me is alive with change — energy forming, scattering, transforming. A child growing, a leaf unfurling, a loved one aging — nothing is ever still. Yet I have often looked at life as if it were a series of snapshots, reacting to moments as if they existed alone.

The truth is that every moment belongs to a larger flow. Like watching a train, I can either fix my gaze on a single compartment or step back to sense its direction, rhythm, and sound. When I see things as part of a continuing sequence, I begin to understand not just where something is, but where it has come from and where it may lead.

I need to make my view dynamic — to recognize the flow that connects past, present, and future. A child growing up will need more care, attention, and love. A person aging will need support and encouragement as their abilities decline. A rose petal opening will invite bees, and when it falls, it will feed the soil that nourishes the next bloom. Seeing life in this way changes how I respond to it — helping me make choices that support what is unfolding. Living in the moment is not pausing time; it is moving with it, aware of change and my place within it.

My Three Invaluable Gifts

I have three gifts that allow me to shape the world around me: the ability to transform energy, to make choices, and to take action. Every time I eat, my body turns food into motion. Every time I think, I turn thought into possibility. Every time I act, I turn intention into reality.

Through these gifts, I participate in the universe's renewal. My choices — what I learn, how I work, whom I care for — create ripples that reach farther than I can see. A well-cooked meal, a piece of writing, a word of appreciation, or an act of kindness — each releases energy that reorders the web around me in small but lasting ways.

These gifts remind me that I am not powerless against entropy. I am part of its balance. Every time I use my energy with awareness, I become both the cause and the continuation of renewal.

Synkria Practices – Working With Entropy

Understanding entropy is only the beginning. Living with it requires practice — learning how to renew, transform, and contribute to the balance of the whole. These tools are not steps to follow but lenses to act through, helping me stay in motion even when life begins to scatter.

Big-Picture Thinking – Seeing the System, Not the Snapshot

To work with entropy, I must learn to see motion, not moments. Every event belongs to a larger pattern in time, space, and cause. Seeing the bigger picture means stepping back — noticing where things began, what has shaped them, and where they may be heading. It takes patience to observe rather than react, but this wider view reveals direction and meaning. From that space, my responses become wiser and more deliberate.

Choose Actions That Renew

Not all actions sustain life — some only consume it. Before acting, I pause to ask: *"What will this renew?"* The answer gives purpose to even the simplest moments — a pause to rest, a conversation to reconnect, a change to refresh routine. Renewal doesn't always look like productivity; sometimes it's stillness that restores strength. Acting with this awareness keeps my energy aligned with what truly matters.

Act for Causes Greater Than Myself

Entropy doesn't just touch me; it moves through everything I'm connected to. When I act for renewal beyond my own circle — to support others, protect the environment, or strengthen community — I restore balance around me and within me. The web I sustain, sustains me in return. Serving a cause greater than myself transforms effort into purpose, and purpose into energy that endures.

These practices are simple but not easy. They ask for awareness, patience, and humility — the willingness to see motion, act with renewal in mind, and remember that I am part of a larger web. Through them, entropy becomes not something to resist but something to move with — a reminder that every end holds the possibility of beginning again.

Synkria: Try Me – Experiencing Entropy and Renewal

Understanding entropy isn't about theory — it's about noticing how life moves, fades, and renews in real time. These simple experiments are ways to observe that movement and participate in its rhythm.

Observe the Drift

Choose something small in your life — a desk, a corner of your room, a potted plant, or even your own mood. For a few days, do nothing to maintain it. Just watch. Notice how disorder slowly appears, how energy disperses on its own.

Then, restore it. Clean, water, nurture, or give attention — and feel how energy flows back, not only into the object or space but also into you.

Ask yourself: How does order feel? What changes when I bring awareness and care?

Energy in Motion

Each day, do one small act that renews something beyond yourself — water a plant, encourage a friend, tidy a shared space, or offer help where it's needed. Do it consciously, knowing that your energy is moving outward, becoming part of something larger.

Later, pause to notice how that act has changed your own state of mind.

Ask yourself: When I renew something around me, what is renewed within me?

The Law of Our Living Body

Our body is an extraordinary network of living systems — intelligent, self-organizing, and largely beyond our conscious control.

She floated upward, yearning to wonder, to walk through clouds and fly with birds. A familiar sound made her turn, and she saw her home — gently breathing and perfectly still.

She saw her heart beat in beautiful symphony, sending energy through unending pathways to distant shores. Lungs swelled and released like waves, an alchemy that changed air into life. Tiny cells pulsed, repaired, remembered, and decided, while a pinkish-grey master looked out, understanding the world. She marvelled at this silent brilliance — a thousand lives working as one.

A sudden wonder filled her — how little she knew of this miracle that carried her, this treasure she was born into. She felt a quiet gratitude, not for something new, but for what had always been hers.

And as she drifted back into herself, she smiled softly — having found her wonder, ready to begin a new relationship with her home, this living intelligence that had loved her all along.

We barely know our own bodies. What we call *ourselves* is mostly a reflection seen through five senses and a mirror. Beneath that surface lies a marvel — a living intelligence that breathes, heals, digests, and feels without our command. It is exquisitely adapted to thrive in its environment, yet fragile beyond it — dependent on the right air, temperature, water, and food.

Built to protect us, the body also protects itself. When neglected or threatened, its alarms sound as anxiety, fear, and stress — reminders that care is not optional but reciprocal. To understand this home of the self is to read the guidebook nature wrote for our well-being.

And what powers this body is not unique to us. The same forces pulse through every living being — energy transforming, cells cooperating, systems self-correcting. Interconnectedness, once again, reveals itself within our own skin. Consider this:

The Intelligence of Cells & Our Distributed Mind - The Body That Thinks Before Thought

You've felt it: the moment when something in you knows before you do. A pause in someone's tone, a flicker in their eyes, and your stomach tightens even before you can explain why. We call it instinct, intuition, a gut feeling—but biology knows it as *the body's first intelligence.*

Interoception is the science behind this quiet knowing. Every second, the body sends millions of internal signals—heartbeat, tension, temperature, breath—to the brain. These signals shape perception before thought even begins. The brain doesn't wait for logic; it listens to the body's data stream and predicts what's coming next.

This predictive loop isn't confined to the skull. The **enteric nervous system,** often called the second brain, runs through the gut with more than a hundred million neurons—more than in the spinal cord. It senses chemical shifts, interprets safety or threat, and sends that information upward through the **vagus nerve,** part of a wider **neurovisceral network** linking gut, heart, and brain. What we call a "gut feeling" is the body's networked intelligence updating its forecast: *safe or unsafe, approach or avoid.*

The process works faster than awareness. **Predictive-processing research** shows that the brain constantly anticipates reality, matching incoming signals from the eyes and ears with internal sensations from the body. When the patterns align, we feel calm. When they clash, we sense unease—sometimes long before we know why. That's why we tense before a raised voice, or feel a surge of certainty that a promise isn't true even when words sound convincing.

Go smaller, and the same logic repeats. **Cellular cooperation** studies reveal that individual cells exchange electrical and chemical messages, adjusting to injury, infection, or imbalance without waiting for conscious instruction. Your tissues repair and adapt through collective decision-making—life solving problems from the inside out.

Our instincts, then, are not mysterious gifts but expressions of this layered intelligence. The body gathers, filters, and predicts; the mind interprets. When we rush, distract, or numb ourselves, we lose access to that data. When we pause—to breathe, to notice tension, to let a feeling speak—we re-enter dialogue with the systems that have protected us since life began.

To listen to the body is not superstition; it's good science. It means respecting the first form of thinking that every living cell still performs: sensing, responding, adapting. The more we learn to hear its signals, the clearer our decisions become—and the closer we move to the quiet competence of life itself.

The Biology of Perception & Consciousness – The World We're Built to See

You miss a message, misread a tone, or stare at your phone while a sunset fades unnoticed. Every day, we confuse the *world as it is* with the *world as we perceive it.* Yet what we experience is not reality itself—it's a filtered construction built by the biology of our senses.

Evolutionary biology tells us our senses evolved for survival, not for truth. Eyes detect only a narrow slice of light; ears hear just a fraction of sound frequencies. Our sensory systems didn't evolve to reveal the universe—they evolved to help us avoid predators, find food, and recognize allies. What we call "reality" is the version of the world most useful for staying alive.

Once signals reach the brain, perception becomes even more selective. **Neuroscientists estimate** that while the body receives about *11 million bits of information every second,* our conscious mind can process only around *forty.* The rest is filtered, compressed, or discarded. Attention acts as a gatekeeper, choosing what to notice and what to ignore. It's why we can drive for miles lost in thought, or fail to hear our name in a noisy room until someone says it with emotion. The brain tunes in and out based on relevance, not accuracy.

Even what we *do* perceive isn't objective. **Predictive-processing theory** shows that perception is the brain's best guess at what's happening. The mind continuously predicts reality, then compares those predictions with sensory input, updating the story in real time. We don't see the world—we experience a constantly edited model of it, shaped by expectation and correction. That's why time can seem to slow in danger, or why two people witnessing the same event remember it differently. Consciousness, in this view, is not a camera—it's a storyteller, weaving survival narratives out of limited data.

And yet, within these limits lies beauty. **Sensory integration research** shows that our brain merges signals from eyes, ears, skin, and balance systems into a coherent experience—the miracle of simply walking without falling, of recognizing a friend's face in dim light. **Neural adaptation** ensures that constant stimuli fade so that change catches our attention: the shift in temperature, a sudden sound, the glint of movement in the grass. The body learns to ignore stability so we can respond to change.

This design keeps us alive—but it also narrows our world. We scroll past moments of wonder because the mind is tuned for urgency, not awe. To see more, we must slow perception down—look longer, listen fully, bring curiosity back to the senses we take for granted. Every pause widens the frame of what our biology allows us to see.

Consciousness, then, isn't the summit of control—it's the meeting point between our body's ancient sensors and the universe they're built to interpret. The world we experience is not the whole world. But when we learn to pay attention, the window grows larger—and life, infinitely richer.

The Biology of Emotion - When Feelings Think for Us

A knot in the stomach before opening bad news. Relief that spreads through the body after finally saying what you meant. A forced smile that, somehow, lightens the moment. Emotion is not just felt in the mind—it begins and ends in the body.

Affective neuroscience shows that emotions started as survival programs long before language or thought. Primitive circuits—what Jaak Panksepp called the SEEK, FEAR, CARE, and PLAY systems—activate specific biological responses: muscles tense, hormones release, breathing shifts. These reactions prepare the organism to move, fight, flee, or connect. Emotion was never decoration; it was instruction.

Over time, evolution wrapped these signals in awareness. The body still speaks first, and the brain interprets afterward. **Antonio Damasio's Somatic Marker Hypothesis** explains how every experience leaves a bodily tag—a rise in pulse, a warmth in the chest, a drop in the gut. When we face a new choice, the body re-creates those sensations to guide decision-making. The nervous system doesn't wait for logic; it remembers through feeling.

This flow runs in both directions. The **autonomic nervous system** sends constant feedback to the brain, and the brain adjusts the body in return.

Anxiety quickens the heart, but slowing the breath calms the mind; sadness collapses posture, yet standing tall can lift mood. **Psychophysiology studies** confirm that changing facial expression or body stance alters hormone levels within minutes—the body teaching the mind how to feel.

Repeated emotions leave physical traces. **Neuroplasticity research** shows that chronic fear, anger, or calm reshape neural networks and even immune function. Emotion becomes habit; chemistry becomes personality. But this also means that awareness, movement, and compassion can rewire those same pathways toward resilience.

So emotion is both input and output—signal and response, messenger and sculptor. It is the body's intelligence translating life into movement. When we pause to feel instead of suppressing, we're not indulging sentiment; we're listening to the oldest operating system we have, one still learning, adapting, and keeping us alive.

The Biology of Pain, Fear, Stress and Anxiety - The Body's Alarm System

A sudden noise, a deadline missed, an argument beginning — and the body reacts before we can think. The heart races, breathing shallows, muscles tighten. These are not random reactions; they are the opening chords of a precise biological symphony built to keep us alive.

At its center is the **HPA axis — the Hypothalamic-Pituitary-Adrenal system.** When the brain perceives threat, the hypothalamus releases chemical messengers to the pituitary gland, which signals the adrenals to flood the body with **adrenaline and cortisol.** Blood moves to the limbs, sugar and oxygen surge, digestion pauses, and awareness narrows. This is the **sympathetic nervous system,** the body's accelerator for fight or flight.

Once safety returns, the **parasympathetic system** should take over — slowing the heart, deepening the breath, restarting digestion. The two systems are meant to work like inhale and exhale, action and recovery. But modern life keeps the accelerator pressed: constant alerts, noise, deadlines, uncertainty. The alarm stays half-on, and the body forgets how to rest.

Psychoneuroimmunology shows what happens then. Chronically elevated cortisol suppresses immunity, increases inflammation, and slows healing. Muscles adapt to constant readiness, storing tension in the neck, jaw, or back. The gut, rich in nerve endings, mirrors our mental state; stress alters digestion and even the composition of the microbiome. Pain and fatigue become the body's language for overload.

The body also remembers. Research into **fascia and somatic memory** finds that chronic stress patterns can linger in connective tissue long after the trigger is gone — a posture of defense that outlives the danger. Repeated activation rewires the brain itself; **neuroplasticity** can make the threat circuits more sensitive, turning ordinary challenges into sources of anxiety.

None of this is failure. Pain, fear, and anxiety are messages, not malfunctions. They say: *pause, breathe, adjust.* The same mechanisms that create distress can create resilience when allowed to complete their cycle. Movement, slow breathing, safe touch, and genuine rest reactivate the parasympathetic response and restore balance. Healing begins the moment the body feels safe enough to turn the alarm off.

Our ancestors relied on this system to survive predators; today, we must learn to survive ourselves — to live in a world our biology never expected, without losing the rhythm of action and recovery that life depends on.

The Biology of Pleasure – The Body's Repair System

After a long walk, you stop and feel a deep sigh leave your body. Laughter loosens your shoulders. Music steadies your breath. These are not small moments; they are the body repairing itself.

Every experience of joy or calm is underpinned by chemistry. **Dopamine** sparks motivation and reward; it rises not just when we receive something pleasant, but when we *anticipate* it—training us to move toward life. **Endorphins** soothe pain and restore ease; a single belly laugh or stretch can release them. **Oxytocin,** sometimes called the bonding hormone, strengthens trust and belonging through touch, empathy, or shared experience. **Serotonin** provides the background stability of well-being, balancing mood and sleep. Together, these molecules form a **reward circuit** connecting the ventral tegmental area, nucleus accumbens, and prefrontal cortex—a loop that reinforces behaviors tied to safety and connection.

Pleasure is the biological counterpoint to stress. Where the **HPA axis** floods the body with cortisol to act, pleasure chemistry signals that the danger has passed. **Polyvagal theory** explains this shift: when the vagus nerve senses safety—through warmth, breath, voice, or gentle social contact—it activates the parasympathetic system, slowing the heart and deepening digestion. The body literally turns from defense to growth.

Inside the brain, **neuroscience of meditation and rest** shows how pleasure also quiets the *default-mode network*—the circuits of self-monitoring and rumination. In that quiet, new connections form; tissues repair; immunity strengthens. Whether through art, prayer, laughter, or affection, the result is the same: the body returns to balance.

Homeostasis is the goal of every living system, and pleasure is one of its tools. After effort or alarm, pleasure closes the loop—confirming that survival succeeded. Ignoring it leaves the cycle unfinished, the body stuck in vigilance. That is why burnout often feels joyless: it's not just fatigue, but the absence of repair chemistry.

Seen through this lens, joy is not indulgence; it is maintenance. A conversation that makes you laugh, sunlight on skin, a shared meal, a song sung aloud—each one tells the body, *you're safe now; you can rebuild.* Pleasure is how life rewards balance and begins again.

Our Personality and Biology – The Blueprint and the Brush

Some people draw energy from silence, others from a room full of voices. One friend stays calm in crisis; another reacts in seconds. We call these differences *personality*, but beneath them lies the quiet influence of biology — the mix of genes, chemistry, and experience that gives each of us our particular traits.

Genetics provides the first sketch. Variations in our neurotransmitter systems — dopamine, serotonin, and noradrenaline — influence how we respond to the world. A more active dopamine system may make one person seek novelty and reward; higher baseline serotonin can create steadiness and optimism. Studies of twins and families show that these differences shape temperament: how easily we excite, soothe, or recover. Biology sets the initial tone of how we meet life.

But genes are not fate. **Epigenetics** shows that experiences can switch genes on or off, altering how they're expressed. Early stress, nurturing, or social safety can change hormone sensitivity and stress response for decades. A calm or caring environment literally writes on our DNA — marks that can even be passed on to the next generation. Our life story becomes a biological echo.

Hormones, too, add color to this picture. **Testosterone and estrogen** influence assertiveness, empathy, and motivation; **oxytocin** deepens trust and bonding. These are not "male" or "female" traits but universal systems of connection and defense, modulated by both biology and context. The same chemistry that sharpens competition can, in another moment, fuel protection and care.

And through it all, the brain remains plastic. **Neuroplasticity** allows repeated behaviors, thoughts, and emotions to strengthen their own pathways. Every time we practice calm, gratitude, or courage, those circuits grow. Personality, then, is not a sculpture but a river — shaped by its source but constantly reshaping its banks.

Understanding this brings compassion. Some of what we judge in others — sensitivity, impatience, reserve — is not choice but wiring. Yet knowing this also gives hope: biology defines potential, not destiny. Awareness, environment, and practice can all redraw the lines.

We are each born with a blueprint, yes — but we hold the brush. Every experience, every act of awareness, is another stroke in the ongoing painting of who we become.

Our Biological Connection with Others – The Web of Life Within and Around Us

You've felt it: the quiet comfort of sitting beside someone who feels safe. A baby's breath slowing to match its mother's. A room softening after shared laughter. These are not just moments of emotion; they are moments of biology — living systems aligning with one another.

At the most fundamental level, we are all made from the same code. **Genetic research** shows that every organism on Earth shares the same molecular alphabet of DNA and RNA. Humans and chimpanzees share 98.8% of their genetic material, while many of our essential genes are identical to those of plants and bacteria. Life did not invent new tools for each species; it refined one shared language, written in four letters, and passed it forward.

Even within our own species, the story is one of continuity. **Mitochondrial DNA,** inherited only through the maternal line, allows every human alive today to trace ancestry back to a single shared lineage — the so-called *Mitochondrial Eve* who lived roughly 150,000 years ago. Every heartbeat, every cell in us, carries echoes of her inheritance. The boundaries between past and present, between "us" and "them," dissolve in biology's long memory.

Connection also happens in real time. **Mirror neurons,** discovered in both primates and humans, fire not only when we act but when we witness someone else acting. They allow us to *feel* another's gesture, to anticipate intent, to empathize. A smile, a yawn, a tear — all travel across this neural bridge, binding individuals into shared experience. Neuroscientists call it **limbic resonance:** the synchronization of emotional states between nervous systems.

The body follows suit. Studies of **bioelectrical and biochemical synchrony** show that people in conversation unconsciously align heart rate, hormone levels, even micro-movements of facial muscles. Our bodies continually negotiate trust and belonging beneath awareness. **Polyvagal theory** adds that the nervous system scans others for cues of safety — tone of voice, eye contact, gesture — and adjusts our own physiology in response. What we call empathy is the biology of mutual regulation.

Even our microbes participate. The **human microbiome** is not a private ecosystem; we exchange microbes through air, touch, food, and shared spaces. Families, friends, even co-workers carry overlapping microbial communities. Our inner worlds are constantly mingling with those around us, blurring the idea of a separate self.

All of this means that connection is not an idea we strive for; it's the condition we live in. Every act of kindness, every shared breath or laugh, reshapes the invisible patterns linking us. To harm another is to disturb our own balance; to nurture is to strengthen the systems that sustain us all.

Individuality, seen this way, is not isolation but expression — one voice in a vast biological choir. The song of life is never solo; it is an ongoing conversation between countless living beings, each responding, adapting, and belonging to the same living whole.

Synkria Reflections: The Gift of My Living Body

My body, a marvel of nature, is a gift I was born with — a living system of breathtaking precision. It walks, runs, heals, digests, balances, grows, and rejuvenates without my command. Its singular purpose is simple yet profound: to keep me alive and well. What a gift indeed.

Yet, like everything in nature, it depends on reciprocity. My body relies on me for nourishment, rest, movement, and care. It trusts me to perceive the world with clarity, to feel without excess, and to allow moments of peace and recovery. As it plays its part in the universal dance of energy — converting, conserving, and releasing — it looks to me for renewal and balance.

Understanding this has redefined my relationship with my own body, leading to six quiet but transformative realizations.

Pleasure Is Renewal

If pleasure is renewal, then joy is the body's way of repairing itself. Yet I rarely give it permission to do so. Modern life glorifies exhaustion — endless work, ambition, and the myth of productivity. We chase achievement while our bodies quietly plead for rest, play, and delight.

Neuroscience reminds us that pleasure is not indulgence but biology's reset. When we laugh, move, or feel awe, dopamine, endorphins, and serotonin course through the brain, signalling the parasympathetic system that it is safe to restore. This cycle — sometimes called the *reward–restoration loop* — closes the stress response that modern life leaves open.

But we often treat fun as something earned rather than required. I once believed that discipline was strength and rest was weakness; now I see that joy is a form of maintenance. The body renews itself not in striving but in ease — in laughter that loosens muscles, in sunlight warming the skin, in moments of curiosity and creation.

To live well, I do not need to save the world or invent anything extraordinary. I need to give my body what it quietly asks for — pleasure, variety, lightness. Renewal begins each time I let myself enjoy the simple act of being alive.

Curiosity Is the Highest Form of Play

I've learned that my mind thrives not only on rest but on discovery. When I challenge myself to learn something new — to read about an unfamiliar idea, solve a problem, or watch a documentary that changes how I see — I feel a spark that no indulgence can match. It is pleasure with depth: curiosity in motion.

Neuroscience explains why. Every time we explore the unknown, the **dopamine reward system** lights up — not as a prize for success but as motivation to keep seeking. The brain rewards exploration itself. In this sense, curiosity is the mind's form of play: it keeps the body alert, flexible, and optimistic. **Neuroplasticity research** shows that novelty literally rewires the brain, building new pathways that slow ageing, sharpen focus, and improve emotional balance.

Modern life often mistakes escape for enjoyment — the drink at the end of a long day, the quick distraction that numbs. But these soothe briefly and leave the body right where it began. True pleasure is engagement, not avoidance. The more I explore, the more alive my biology feels; curiosity is fuel, not relief.

Every act of learning, every moment of wonder, tells my body that it is still growing. Curiosity stretches the mind and renews the chemistry of joy. To explore, to question, to play with ideas — this is how life keeps itself interested in living.

The Flexible Self – Biology Follows Belief

I've often described myself with limits: *I'm not athletic. I'm not outgoing. I can't do that.* These labels feel like self-knowledge, but they're really small cages — instructions my mind gives my body about what is possible. The truth is, the body listens.

Neuroscience shows that belief is not a metaphor — it's circuitry. The brain's networks for imagination and action overlap; when I *believe* I can do something, the same neurons fire as when I actually attempt it. Repetition of thought becomes rehearsal for reality. Over time, **neuroplasticity** wires these patterns into habit, shaping both performance and personality.

Even my genetic and hormonal systems are not fixed. **Epigenetics** reveals that experience can turn genes on or off, influencing emotion, confidence, and adaptability. Every time I face something new with openness rather than fear, I am teaching my biology to respond differently the next time.

The idea that "I am this" and "not that" is comforting — it simplifies life — but it's false. The body is built to adapt, not to obey identity. When danger arises, it runs; when needed, it heals; when inspired, it creates. My personality is not a prison; it's a current, always changing shape with experience.

When I stop defining myself by the past and meet each moment as it is, my body responds with fresh intelligence. Biology follows belief — not blind optimism, but trust in my innate capacity to become what the moment needs.

Expression Is Release – Letting Emotion Move Through

There are moments when music starts and my body wants to move — a beat, a sway, an urge to join — but my mind hesitates. I look around, wondering who might be watching, and I stop myself. The song ends, and so does something inside me. Later, I feel an odd sadness, as if I missed more than a dance. I've learned this isn't about the music at all. It's about emotion withheld.

Affective neuroscience tells us that emotion begins as movement — electrical and chemical currents preparing the body for action. **Psychoneuroimmunology** shows what happens when that action is blocked: energy meant to flow stays trapped, raising stress hormones and inflammation. What we call "bottling up" is quite literal; tension lodges in muscles, fascia, and breath.

Expression, then, is not indulgence — it's regulation. When we speak honestly, cry, laugh, dance, or even breathe deeply, we are completing biological cycles that the body started. The act of feeling is the body's way of restoring balance. **Somatic therapies** have found that allowing physical expression during emotion lowers cortisol and restores immune strength faster than suppression does.

Walls built around feeling do not hold it in; they hold it *with us.* The tide of emotion never stops — it only waits. Each time I allow sadness to pass through, or joy to rise fully, the body releases what it was carrying. Expression becomes intelligence — a message fully delivered.

My body doesn't need me to fix its feelings; it needs me to let them move through. In that surrender lies clarity, healing, and peace.

The Healing Power of Belonging

There's a certain energy I feel when I'm with others — in a gym, on a walk, or even among strangers at a concert. My body feels lighter, movements easier, spirit higher. It's not just mood; it's biology responding to connection.

Neuroscience and social biology show that we are wired for togetherness. When we move, laugh, or share moments with others, our **mirror neurons** fire in synchrony. The body begins to match rhythms, postures, even micro-expressions — a silent language of belonging. This synchrony triggers oxytocin and endorphins, lowering stress hormones and restoring calm. **Studies in**

vagal tone — the measure of how balanced our nervous system is — reveal that it improves when we engage socially, even briefly.

The truth is simple: isolation is not our natural state. Our ancestors survived by being part of a tribe, and our biology still believes that safety is found in connection.

A shared smile, a morning jog with a friend, even a conversation with a kind stranger — all of these remind the body that it is not alone in the world.

I used to think healing meant solitude and silence; now I see that sometimes it means company — to be seen, mirrored, understood. My body thrives in presence, not just in rest.

Togetherness is not a luxury; it is how life remembers itself.

Alignment Brings Renewal – The Science of Flow and Letting Go

There are moments when I am fully absorbed in what I love — writing, creating, walking, or even cooking — and time seems to dissolve. Thought quiets, effort disappears, and I feel deeply alive. **Neuroscientists call this the flow state,** when the thinking brain softens and the body takes over with seamless coordination. In this state, heart, breath, and movement fall into quiet coherence — a biological harmony that restores rather than drains.

For years, I chased success the way I was taught — achievement, status, validation. It left me exhausted and oddly detached. My biology didn't recognise these as signs of safety or meaning; it only understood peace, engagement, and joy. To my body, purpose isn't a goal. It's a state of coherence — when what I do, think, and feel move in the same direction.

Letting go of social conditioning is not rebellion; it's repair. Every time I release an old story — about who I should be, or what I must achieve — the body exhales, cells recalibrate, and energy returns. This is how healing happens: not by adding more, but by allowing life to flow as it was designed to.

Our bodies also hold the emotions of our past experiences — the laughter of a happy marriage, the fear of a childhood wound, the grief of loss. The mind may forget details, but the body remembers the feeling. An experience cannot be undone, but the emotion attached to it can be released. When I stop reliving old stories and allow these feelings to move through, the body lightens, clarity returns, and healing begins.

When I am aligned, my body recognises itself again. Renewal isn't an act of will — it's the natural consequence of being in tune with my own living intelligence.

Synkria Practises – Living in Harmony With My Body

The body I inhabit is a living intelligence — sensing, repairing, renewing. It listens closely to how I live, what I think, and what I allow myself to feel. To live well within it, I need to work *with* it, not *on* it. Here are four ways I practise that partnership every day:

Treat Pleasure, Letting Go, and Sleep as Medicine

Each day, I make space for simple pleasures — a short nap, a walk in sunlight, a moment of laughter, or a few minutes of music I love. I allow myself to feel joy without guilt. I release what no longer matters, and for what does, I decide on clear actions and let it rest there. I guard my eight hours of sleep like medicine. Pleasure, letting go, and sleep are how my body repairs itself.

Do Something Physical With Others

More than just catching up, I like to move with others — walk with a neighbour, stretch together, play a game, exercise, or cook with my family. I notice how my body relaxes when it moves beside others, even strangers; breath, pace, and energy begin to synchronize. Shared movement releases warmth and ease that solitude rarely brings. When I move with others, my body remembers that it belongs.

Understand the Language of Emotions

When a strong feeling arises — irritation, craving, or sadness — I try not to go with my first reaction. Instead, I pause and ask, *What is my body trying to tell me?* Over time, I've realized that a craving for sweets is often my body's way of saying, *I need dopamine to recover.* So I create something instead, and the craving fades.

If I feel stiff, I stretch, breathe, or step outside. When I feel love, I express it fully. When I feel joy, I show it in my smile. Sometimes the message is clear — expression — but often, it hides in deeper layers. Learning the language of emotions is the greatest gift I've given myself.

Change the Question From "Who Am I?" to "What Have I Not Tried Today?"

I am in motion — learning, growing, changing — and so the answer to *Who am I?* shifts every day. Instead, I ask, *What have I not tried today?* I don't mind being easily bored; I see seeking new things as exploration — not just of the world but of myself. Each new experience reveals more of my versatility, my capabilities, my potential for growth. Novelty wakes up my brain, brightens my mood, and reminds me that I am still growing — keeping pace with both who I am and who I can become.

Synkria Try Me – The Law of Your Living Body

Understanding your body is one thing; feeling its intelligence is another.

These simple *Try Me* moments help you bridge that gap — small pauses that invite you to listen, connect, and renew right where you are.

The Pleasure Scan

Pause for a few seconds and notice what would bring you a small pleasure right now — a sip of water, sunlight on your skin, stretching your back, or humming a tune. Do it immediately.

Your body reads this as safety and begins to repair itself.

The Synchrony Moment

If someone is nearby, match your walking pace or breathing rhythm to theirs for a few moments. If you're alone, tune in to a natural rhythm — your heartbeat, your steps, or the sound of the wind.

Synchrony reminds your body that it is part of something larger.

The Emotion Check-In

Close your eyes and ask, *What am I feeling right now? Where do I feel it in my body?* Don't analyse — just name it: *tightness, warmth, calm, restlessness.*

The simple act of naming lowers stress hormones and brings clarity.

These tiny pauses are how you remind your body that you're listening. Awareness becomes medicine, and life begins to move with ease.

The Law of Equilibrium

The oscillation between opposing forces is life

She sat on her terrace in the calm of morning, sunlight warming her face, a soft breeze brushing her skin. It was her first attempt at meditation, and she couldn't understand how paying attention to something as ordinary as breath could bring balance and peace. Still, she tried.

Inhale. Exhale.

Slowly, the world around her began to widen. Each breath felt like a gentle swing — between taking in and letting go, between fullness and emptiness. It had done this since birth, without permission or command. In that quiet moment, something vast revealed itself: nothing in life can stay on one side for long. Life is not the inhale or the exhale, but the motion between them.

Then she realised — her breath was not hers alone. It was part of a vast exchange that bound her to the garden, the planet, and the stars that forged the oxygen she now held. Balance lived everywhere — in breath and breeze, in giving and receiving, in the quiet, endless movement that sustains all things.

As she breathed again, the ordinary morning felt changed. The air seemed larger, alive with meaning. For the first time, she wasn't just breathing — she was participating. Balance wasn't an idea anymore; it was her.

Everything in existence — living or not — moves in cycles between opposing forces, from birth to death. "Now" is simply where we are in that cycle. Life unfolds in the oscillation between extremes: day and night, fire and water, joy and sorrow, fear and courage. Even our smallest experiences rest on this motion — giving and receiving, holding and releasing, rising and falling. Most of our life objectives are about moving from one state to another— from poor to rich, from not knowing to knowledgeable, from discomfort to comfort. This constant movement between counterbalancing forces is existence. Consider the following:

The Birth of the Universe — Creation in Balance

The universe began not from chaos but from balance — a delicate tension between expansion and gravity. Expansion flung matter outward; gravity gathered it back, shaping stars, galaxies, and time itself. Too much of either, and nothing would have held together.

That same law of balance continues within every atom. A positive nucleus pulls in negative electrons, attraction meeting resistance, forming structure from opposites. From galaxies to grains of dust, from atoms to breath, existence persists only because opposing forces learn to share the same space.

Earth's Equilibrium — The Delicate Balance of Life

The same dance continues closer to home. Earth thrives because it sits in the narrow "Goldilocks zone" — not too hot, not too cold. Our molten core generates a magnetic shield that protects us from solar radiation. Plate tectonics recycle carbon, stabilizing the atmosphere and keeping the planet breathable.

But the balance is fragile. Ocean temperatures, forests, and gases all maintain a network of checks and counterchecks. Carbon dioxide warms Earth just enough to sustain life; too much, and the scale tips into catastrophe. A single degree of warming can alter currents, amplify storms, and drown coasts.

In nature, predator and prey also maintain this equilibrium. Lions keep antelope herds healthy; antelopes, through their grazing and movement, keep grasslands alive. No species thrives in isolation. But humans, with our technology and expansion, have stepped outside this natural rhythm. The further we move from nature's feedback loops, the more we test the very equilibrium that sustains us.

Systems — Balance in Motion

What holds true for nature holds true for our systems. Economies thrive with demand and supply, production and consumption. When balanced, they sustain livelihoods and progress; when they tilt, they spiral into inflation or collapse.

Societies, too, rest on counterweights. Democracy is balance institutionalized — opposing voices, alternate ideas, diverse beliefs kept in motion so no one force dominates. When extremes silence moderation, conflict erupts. Balance is not absence of tension; it is tension held in balance.

The Mind — Between Solitude and Society

Inside us, the same pendulum swings. The human mind needs solitude for reflection, yet craves connection for meaning. Neuroscientists studying social cognition have shown that the same brain circuits that process physical pain light up during loneliness. Psychologist Julianne Holt-Lunstad found that chronic social isolation increases the risk of premature death by over 25%.

We survive by moving between these poles — retreat and return, thought and conversation, silence and sharing. A healthy mind is one that keeps this motion alive.

The Body — Homeostasis and Heart Coherence

Our bodies are balance in motion. Through homeostasis, we regulate temperature, hydration, and hormones — constantly adjusting to internal and external changes. The nervous system itself is a living seesaw: the sympathetic (alert, stress, action) branch prepares us for action, the parasympathetic (rest, recovery, healing) restores.

Modern research deepens this understanding through *heart coherence.* The heart has its own neural network, communicating with the brain via biochemical and electromagnetic signals. When breathing, emotions, and heart rhythms synchronize, the body enters a coherent state — calm yet alert, centered yet dynamic. Relaxation releases tension; but coherence harmonizes it. In this micro-equilibrium, heart and mind no longer compete but collaborate. Stress becomes movement rather than fracture — a pendulum swinging smoothly, not snapping.

The Pendulum — The Rhythm of Balance

Physics gives us a simple mirror: the pendulum. It swings endlessly between opposites, never still yet always in rhythm. The midpoint is not rest but return — the reminder that every extreme carries within it the pull of its opposite. Life, too, finds balance not by avoiding opposites but by learning to move gracefully between them.

Yin and Yang — Ancient Echoes of Balance

Long before modern science, Eastern philosophy captured this truth in the symbol of Yin and Yang: light within dark, dark within light, each containing the seed of the other. Science, from cosmology to neuroscience, now echoes the wisdom traditions intuited — opposites are not enemies but partners. Balance is the art of sustaining their dance.

Equilibrium, then, is not the stillness of perfection but the steady rhythm of adaptation — a harmony that is constantly being tuned, within us and around us.

Synkria Reflections: What Equilibrium Means in My Life

As I reflected on balance, I saw my own life—like everyone else's—as a pendulum, always in motion between opposites: gains and losses, joys and sorrows. Challenging periods are followed by seasons of peace and abundance. My outcomes are shaped by the balance of my strengths and weaknesses. I realised that most of my goals were not about progress, but about restoring what felt out of balance.

Over time, I began to see balance not as something occasional but as the constant backdrop of living. It was never about perspective—seeing the glass half full or half empty. The truth is that the glass is both – half full and half empty. To see balance, I must see the whole glass, not just the half I prefer. Balance is not a pause in motion; it is the motion itself.

The Mind Measures, the Heart Gives Meaning

When logic and emotion move together, something changes. A morning walk can be about steps counted and calories burned—or it can also be about the rustle of leaves, the dragonflies in sunlight, the smile of a stranger, the smell of rain—and the walk becomes a pleasant memory.

For years, I feared opening my heart; it is prone to getting hurt, and that vulnerability felt unsafe, so I let my mind take over. But life grew mechanical and joyless. When I allowed the heart to walk beside the mind, even the smallest routines—watering plants, greeting a neighbour, cooking dinner—became memories. My life is all a set of memories, made when my mind and heart were in balance. The mind measures the walk; the heart makes it meaningful.

My Actions Can Restore Balance

Each action adds weight to one side of life's scale. Planting a tree, calming an angry voice, feeding someone hungry, showing kindness—each steadies the world a little. Those who act for needs greater than their own—volunteers, caregivers, conservationists—help restore the balance we all depend on. Their actions, however small, ripple outward in ways they may never see.

Balance is not just a social responsibility but a personal one too. To earn money but also spend time with family. To live sustainably yet contribute to causes that protect nature. To nurture personal hobbies yet care for the community I live in. In all that I do, balance asks me to remember: I am both an individual and part of a whole.

Listening to Emotion and Logic

My heart wants to go on an unaffordable vacation; my mind says I can't. I live through this conflict often—between impulse and reason, indulgence and restraint. It's common sense not to binge, overspend, or overwork, yet I find myself guilty of all three.

Following emotion alone often ends in guilt, while following logic alone feels like compromise. For a long time, I thought balance meant choosing the wiser side. But equilibrium has taught me otherwise—it isn't about which side wins, but how they take turns to lead. When I allow each its rightful moment, they begin to cooperate. Emotion gives energy; logic gives direction. Together, they restore balance.

Sometimes balance happens in silence, before a choice is even made. When anger rises and I pause long enough to breathe, I can feel the swing begin to slow. The breath steadies the heart, the heart steadies the thought, and the mind finds its way back to center. In that instant, I am both the swing and the still point — motion and calm existing together. Balance is not something I find; it is something that finds me when I stop resisting motion.

Every Coin Has Two Sides, and Both Belong to Me

If I welcome abundance, I must also welcome challenge, because they are inseparable. Growth requires discomfort; success demands courage; love asks for compromise. If I am unwilling to accept both sides, I must let go of the coin itself. Equilibrium asks me not to choose, but to hold.

When I hold the coin this way, I also find comfort in knowing that challenging times will be followed by abundance, and sorrow will give way to joy. Balance reminds me that both are temporary, both essential. The art is not in holding on to either, but in learning to let each have its turn.

I Can't Have Everything, but I Can Have Some Part of Everything

Balance means something is always missing. This simply translates to—I can't have everything. This is not cruelty but design. No one is meant to have it all. Life moves by leaving behind as new things arrive. If I had everything, struggle would vanish, and soon so would meaning. Struggle gives meaning. That, too, is balance.

But it also means I can have *some* part of everything. A relationship becomes perfect not when it is flawless, but when listening, patience, and compromise co-exist. Success comes when ambition is in harmony with skill and effort. Joy deepens when I learn to let go. As artists have known for millennia, the perfect sculpture is the imperfect one—the asymmetry that makes it alive.

Synkria Practises – What Can I Do to Restore Balance?

Standing inside a life that is motion between opposites, I ask: what can I actually do? I cannot stop the pendulum from moving, but I can learn how to move with it.

Synkria offers two tools — two halves of the whole. One helps me find outer equilibrium, the other restores inner equilibrium. Together, they teach me how to move in harmony with life's rhythm — to float when life expands, and to act when clarity returns.

Outer Equilibrium – Float Like a Butterfly, Sting Like a Bee

Muhammad Ali's rhythm was more than athletic brilliance — it was balance in motion. Float when life throws punches you cannot control; sting when an opening appears.

When I stop resisting what's unpredictable, I conserve energy. I learn to adapt, observe, and let situations pass through me. And when the moment arrives that calls for decisive action, I strike — not from panic, but from precision.

Equilibrium asks for both: the lightness to move with uncertainty and the strength to act when timing aligns. Balance is not being still; it's knowing when to dance and when to deliver.

Inner Equilibrium – Align Head and Heart

The mind seeks order; the heart seeks wonder. When one dominates, life tips off balance.

The practice is simple — in every choice, let both speak. When my mind makes a plan, I pause to ask if my heart feels at peace with it. When my heart desires something deeply, I let my mind check if it's grounded in reality.

Over time, this dialogue becomes seamless — thought and feeling no longer pull apart, they move together. When head and heart act in concert, balance becomes effortless. Decisions become clear, relationships softer, and life regains its rhythm.

These two practices — outer and inner — are how I stay in motion without losing my center. They turn balance from an idea into a way of life, one that lets me flow through life without falling out of step.

Synkria – Try Me

If balance is a way of life, its practice begins in the small moments of every day. Here are two simple ways to experience equilibrium in motion.

Practice One: Seeing the Other Side

Pick one area of your life today where you feel pulled to extremes—work, food, emotion. Pause, breathe, and name both sides before deciding what would restore balance.

Ask yourself: *What needs to shift right now for equilibrium to return?* Sometimes it's action; sometimes it's letting go.

Practice Two: Balance Is Motion, Not Stillness

When you feel stress rise, take three slow breaths, noticing the swing: inhale (expansion), exhale (release).

In that simple rhythm lies the reminder that balance is never a pause—it is the movement that keeps us alive.

The Law of Interconnectedness

Every ripple finds its way back

On a Thursday evening, a woman in a city you'll never visit missed her train. She sighed, bought a tea, and messaged a friend to say she'd be late.

The friend, waiting outside a small theatre, passed his extra ticket to a stranger who happened to be there because a meeting had ended early.

The stranger, who had been thinking of quitting a job, met the actor after the play and decided to stay one more month. In that month, she designed a product that ended up in your hands two years later.

You didn't know her. She didn't know you. But a missed train, a paper cup of tea, a borrowed hour—these moved the web that moved you.

You are part of an unimaginably vast, intricate web where every action, cause, and effect is interwoven — endlessly influencing everything else. Nothing in this universe moves alone. Nothing is without consequence.

Science, across every field — from physics to biology to human behavior — has been revealing this truth for centuries: everything connects.

Relativity — We Share One Fabric

Einstein showed that space and time are not separate things but a single fabric — spacetime — curved by matter and energy. The galaxies wheeling across a night sky are not ornaments hung elsewhere; they are part of the same cloth that holds you.

You live inside the universe the way a thread lives inside a tapestry. The distant pulls of stars, the patient drift of planets, the gravity that keeps your feet on the ground — all of it belongs to one woven field.

To say *"I am here"* is also to say *"I am in it"* — within the same fabric that binds distant galaxies to this breathing, ordinary moment.

Ecosystems — The Rain on My Roof Is a Chorus

Bees disappear, and orchards fade. Forests thin, and the rains change their habits. Soil loses its living richness, and rivers turn sullen and brown. The water in my glass is not only a local gift; it is the end of a long negotiation among oceans, winds, forests, mountains, and microbes.

When the web is healthy, rain knows its way home. When we loosen even one strand, we feel it in our harvest, in our prices, in the taste of our food. I might never see the forest that waters me — yet it is there, quietly paying my bills.

Thermodynamics and the Sun — I Carry a Star in Me

Energy is not created or destroyed; it only changes form. The warmth on my cheek this morning began in the sun's core, where hydrogen fuses into helium in a white-hot forge. That light crossed space, woke a leaf, entered a fruit, and became the strength in my legs, the spark in my thoughts.

To eat is to borrow sunlight. To breathe is to spend it. I am, quite literally, a walking continuation of a star.

Quantum Entanglement — A Mystery We Already Recognize

In 1972, John Clauser and Stuart Freedman confirmed what Einstein called "spooky action at a distance": entanglement. Two particles, once linked, continue to respond to each other no matter how far apart they drift — as if distance were a rumor, not a rule.

It sounds impossible until I notice how often I sense a dear one's mood before a message arrives, how laughter catches across a room like flame, how grief makes strangers lower their voices on the same day.

Perhaps physics only names what life already shows us: connection can be instant, and sometimes explanation follows experience.

Six Degrees and Social Networks — Strangers Carry Our Future

Frigyes Karinthy imagined, and modern networks confirm, that we are separated by only a few steps. A friend of a friend opens a door. A message travels farther than we intend. Opportunity and danger both move along these hidden roads.

Each connection carries potential far beyond intention — an unseen network of participation that evolution itself depends on. I do not walk alone; I travel in a crowd I cannot see.

Mirror Neurons — The Face I Wear Writes on Your Day

In the 1990s, Giacomo Rizzolatti's team described mirror neurons — cells that fire both when I act and when I watch you act. This is why a yawn spreads, why you stand taller when others do, why kindness can rewire a morning. Your nervous system is porous: it lets the world in, and the world lets you in.

The Golden Ratio — Patterns That Prefer Harmony

The golden ratio, $\Phi \approx 1.618$, appears from the spiral of a nautilus to the swirls of cyclones and galaxies, from branching trees to designs we find pleasing. Artists have used it for centuries because it feels right in the body.

Some human proportions often echo it — the span from shoulder to forearm, the layout of facial features, the taper of limbs. It's nature's quiet reminder that harmony isn't learned — it's remembered.

Fields and Shared Mind — The Edge of Knowing

Franz Anton Mesmer once spoke of a connecting "animal magnetism" — an idea long abandoned, yet it echoes a deep human intuition: that we affect one another in ways beyond measure.

The Global Consciousness Project at Princeton found odd statistical patterns in random number generators during major world events — results debated, but still intriguing. Even if the data remains uncertain, it reminds me that emotion and attention can move across distance faster than logic can explain. When minds align, the world often stirs.

Karma and Reincarnation — Threads Across Time

Long before laboratories, traditions spoke of cause and consequence that outlive a moment, even a lifetime. Karma sees every action as ripening; reincarnation imagines that life continues its lesson.

Together they suggest an interconnectedness not only in the present but braided across millennia — past feeding present, present feeding future. Whether taken as faith or metaphor, they press upon one enduring question: *What am I sending forward?*

Synkria reflections - What Interconnectedness Means in My Life

Interconnectedness is written everywhere — in the sky, the soil, within our cells, across our friendships, and perhaps through time itself. Which led me to a quieter question that no laboratory could answer: *What does all this mean for my own life?*

I Influence Everything, and Everything Influences Me

Every word I speak, every choice I make, every mood I carry creates ripples. A curt reply can shrink a day; a patient silence can give it room to breathe. These ripples do not stop where I stop — they pass through people I will never meet, altering routes I will never walk.

And just as I influence, I am influenced — by the stranger's kindness, by a forest I will never see that pulls rain from the sky, by the fragile good work of countless hands that make my ordinary day possible.

I am not insignificant, and I am not alone.

Nothing Is Random

What I call "random" is often only what I cannot see. A harvest fails — somewhere, years ago, a forest was cut, a sea warmed by a fraction, a wind turned, a policy was delayed. I catch a cold; a thousand small timings align.

If I could see the web in its fullness, surprise would soften into recognition. This is not to deny the shock of events; it is to understand that shock lives inside a pattern.

Actions and Results Are Not Directly Proportional

This is why life can feel "unfair." I may labor and lose; someone else may be careless and win. Outcomes are the intersection of countless ripples, not the straight reward of my effort alone.

That truth can wound — or it can free. It frees me when I remember: my domain is my action, not the outcome. I act as well as I can, and then meet the result — whatever it is — with willingness to act again.

I am Interdependent

My independence is a beautiful myth. I live on loans: sunlight, water, language, infrastructure, trust. Even my body is a federation — trillions of cells and microbes keeping silent promises on my behalf.

Interdependence is not a weakness; it is the ordinary condition of being alive. The wiser question is not *"How can I avoid dependence?"* but *"How can I make my dependencies healthy, just, and kind?"*

Purpose Is Common — I Find It by Playing My Part

An interconnected reality does not spin in chaos. It leans toward a common good — survival, sustainability, and growth. Herds in nature move this way. Togetherness protects each member, ensures food, wards off predators. The rhythm of the herd may look repetitive, even dull, but it is what sustains life.

Each member carries responsibility: keep pace, hold formation, play your part. When one strays, the whole becomes weaker, and every member more vulnerable.

In my interconnected world, purpose is not a distant treasure to be found — it is shared. The herd's purpose becomes mine. My task is to walk with it, to contribute to its rhythm, to play the role that is mine to play.

This purpose is not always grand. It hides in the smallest, most ordinary actions. When I water a garden, I sustain not just plants but an unseen network of soil microbes, birds, and bees. When I raise responsible children, I strengthen the herd for a future I will not live to see. When I keep peace in my family, I add strength to the whole.

Purpose lives here — in the daily, mundane, sometimes boring work of sustaining life around me. And when I act with this awareness, something shifts. Purpose finds me — in every watering can, every quiet kindness, every task repeated without applause. These actions, small as they seem, are threads in the great fabric of survival and growth.

To play my part is not to lose myself, but to discover myself within the whole. It gives me strength, clarity, and even joy.

I Have to Play My Part

If I am a thread in a web, then the way I pull matters. Most of the web leans toward life: the sun keeps its appointment, seeds remember how to split, strangers keep trying.

My part is to return what I receive — to contribute more order than I consume, more kindness than I borrow, more repair than I require.

Synkria Practices – What Can I Control?

Standing inside a living web, it's natural to ask: *What can I actually do to influence this world for the better?* I cannot command outcomes — they belong to the web. But Synkria offers three tools I can hold in my hands.

Ask — What Does This Impact?

Every choice I make sends ripples through the web. When I pause to ask *"What does this impact?"* I widen my field of awareness. This question doesn't guarantee foresight, but it trains the mind to sense patterns — to glimpse how one act can branch into many consequences.

When I can't control outcomes, I can still shape intention. I may not predict where the ripples will reach, but I move with clarity and calm, prepared to meet whatever returns.

The web may not yield the result I prefer, but it always responds to mindful action.

Hope — Trust the Web's Quiet Tilt Toward Life

Hope is not prediction; it is permission to keep acting. The world is not neutral. Every morning the cosmos spends itself on our behalf: light returns, breath arrives, strangers keep their silent agreements.

To practice hope is to notice this generosity and join it. It steadies me when results disappoint, and it keeps my actions from shrinking into cynicism. Hope is courage stretched between what *is* and what *could be.*

Collaboration — Move With, Not Against

Because I am interdependent, my flourishing is braided with yours. Collaboration is the art of aligning threads — asking for help, offering it freely, designing systems that multiply care and reduce harm.

When we build together, our individual limitations become the web's strength. Collaboration is how a personal intention becomes a public good.

With these tools, I can move from fear to confidence, from isolation to belonging. I begin to see my life not as a random accident but as a thread in a great design — fragile yet vital, small yet indispensable.

Synkria – Try Me

Synkria takes practice. Each law is easier to understand when lived, even in small ways.

Here are two simple practices to begin with. They don't require extra time — only a shift in awareness. Each one is a way of living the law right now. These small exercises will get you started and prepare you to apply it to bigger experiences.

Practice One: Trace the Invisible Web Behind a Single Action

When you drink your morning tea or coffee, pause and observe: Who grew it? Who harvested, transported, or packaged it? Who made the cup that holds it?

Let yourself notice the network of lives hidden in one sip — an unseen web of effort that connects distant hands to your morning.

Practice Two: Notice How Your Words Ripple

Today, choose one person you interact with and give them your full attention. Listen with empathy — no phone, no hurry, no assumptions.

Notice how even a few minutes of true presence change the interaction, the mood, and perhaps the rest of their day.

The Law of Evolution

Our species is progressing — at great cost. Yet we, its individuals, have forgotten how. Evolution needs harmony — and individual participation.

He had walked for hours through the forest, phone dead, trail long lost. At first there was irritation — then fear — and finally, a kind of surrender. He sat beside a stream, and in searching for hope, began to notice the life all around him.

A tree had split stone to reach water, its bark etched with the memory of storms. Leaves turned toward slivers of light, patient in their ascent. A butterfly drifted past, escaping the quick tongue of a frog. Nearby, a spider wove its web — a design refined and remembered over millions of years. Above them, clouds pushed across the mountain, breaking apart to give the forest rain.

Everywhere around him, he noticed the harmony of struggle, learning, growth, and participation. In a place where he was lost, all other life listened, adjusted, and remembered how to belong.

He felt, suddenly, like the outsider — the one creature that no longer knew how to find its way without direction.

When he finally rose, he did not look for the trail. He listened instead — ready to participate, to learn. He knew now he would find his way home.

In the forest, evolution felt alive — not as history, but as presence. Every leaf, insect, and cloud seemed to carry an ancient knowing: to listen, to learn, to adapt. We often think of evolution as a tale of fossils and time, but it is unfolding in every moment, in every act of harmony. The same intelligence that shaped wings and roots still shapes us. Yet, somewhere along the way, we mistook progress for evolution — growing outward as a species while forgetting how to grow inward as individuals. To understand what it truly means to evolve, we must look again at the science of adaptation, cooperation, and participation — and see how life continues to refine itself through participation.

Evolution Happens Through Connections

Every living system on Earth evolved by staying connected to something larger than itself. Trees make food with sunlight, soil, and air; they reproduce without seeking pleasure and help other life forms to sustain.

Modern evolutionary biology describes this through **coevolution** — species evolving together in response to one another. Flowers and pollinators are a perfect example. Over millions of years, plants refined their colours, scents, and nectar to attract specific insects, while those insects evolved specialized tongues or flight patterns to reach them. Each species became what it is because of the other.

Humans, too, are products of this connected intelligence. Yet, as a species, we have drifted from this law of connection. Most of us can no longer name the trees in our streets, sense direction without GPS, or understand the weather cycles that feed us. This makes us more dependent, not more evolved.

We must rediscover our connections to nature — evolution has always been a shared act. We grow not through dominance, but through belonging.

Struggle as Nature's Teacher

In nature, every leap in evolution begins with struggle. When environments change, life must respond — or perish. This relentless testing is how new strengths, instincts, and forms emerge.

Animals adapt through movement and necessity. When drought strikes, elephants remember ancient water paths across deserts. Each migration refines their collective memory and social intelligence. The wildebeests that cross the Serengeti every year face exhaustion, predators, and hunger, yet their journey ensures renewal — they find fresh grass, feed others along the way, and return stronger.

Scientists call this **adaptive pressure** — the process by which stress and challenge drive evolution. Species that endure moderate struggle grow more resilient, while those that face none lose their edge. It is struggle, not comfort, that refines life's intelligence.

Humans are no different. Our struggles have simply moved inward — into the realms of society, ambition, and meaning. We learn and adapt through these pressures, building complex systems to protect and progress as a collective. Yet, while these struggles shape behaviour within our societies, they have also led the collective itself to move towards imbalance and self-destruction. To evolve further, our struggles must once again align with the larger world — with nature, the planet, and the universe that hold us.

Evolution's quiet truth is this — every struggle, rightly understood, is an invitation to grow in harmony with life itself.

Cooperation — Nature's Secret Engine: How Participation Sustains Evolution

For most of life's history, evolution has been described as a battle for survival. But beneath competition lies a deeper truth — cooperation is what sustains life.

The cells in our bodies are living proof. Billions of years ago, simple single-celled organisms began merging and sharing their strengths. One cell learned to process sunlight, another to break down oxygen; together, they created the first complex cells — a partnership known in biology as **symbiogenesis.** Every breath we take still depends on that ancient act of cooperation.

In nature, cooperation appears everywhere. Ant colonies build vast networks where each individual plays a precise role. Bees communicate through dances to guide the hive to food sources. Coral reefs thrive through countless species living in mutual dependence — fish cleaning parasites, algae feeding corals, corals sheltering fish. Evolution rewards systems that share, because shared strength is survival multiplied.

Humans are no exception. Our greatest leaps — language, agriculture, cities, science — all emerged through collaboration. Yet, our modern instinct has shifted from *what can I give to what can I gain.* When individuals withdraw their participation, the collective weakens. Cooperation is not charity; it is evolution's method of preserving balance.

Life does not move forward through competition, but through contribution. Evolution's secret engine is not rivalry — it is relationship.

The Entropy of Progress — When Evolution Outruns Balance

In nature, growth that ignores balance always collapses. When algae bloom unchecked on a lake, they consume oxygen and kill the life beneath them—only to die themselves. Forests that over-grow without periodic fire eventually choke their own renewal. Evolution depends as much on restraint as on expansion.

Science explains this through **ecological feedback loops.** Every ecosystem regulates itself through limits—predators keeping prey in check, soil replenishing slowly, rainfall setting the pace for growth. When these loops break, entropy takes over. Collapse isn't failure; it's nature's correction.

Human progress has followed a similar path. Our population, industries, and technologies expand faster than the planet's capacity to renew. We measure advancement by speed and scale, not balance. The result is a civilization evolving collectively but decaying ecologically—an intelligence outpacing its own wisdom.

True evolution learns to self-regulate. Growth that listens endures; growth that consumes destroys. When progress outruns harmony, evolution turns upon itself.

From Genes to Memes — The Evolution of Ideas

Evolution is no longer confined to biology. In humans, the process of inheritance and adaptation has shifted from genes to ideas. Thoughts, beliefs, and stories now behave like living entities — spreading, mutating, competing, and surviving across generations.

Biologist Richard Dawkins first described this as **memetic evolution** — where cultural units of information, or "memes," act like genes, replicating through imitation and communication. From language and religion to technology and art, our creations evolve through variation and selection. The ideas that survive are those that adapt to the minds and moods of the time.

But unlike genes, memes don't always serve collective well-being. Falsehoods, fear, and division can spread faster than truth, shaping societies in ways biology never could. Our capacity for shared imagination — the same force that built civilization — can also destabilize it.

To evolve consciously, we must curate what we pass on. Each thought, story, and creation contributes to the mental ecosystem of humanity. Evolution now unfolds not only in our bodies, but in our ideas.

The future is not written in our genes — it is written in what we choose to share.

Evolution Has No Favorites — Continuance Is Never Guaranteed

Evolution does not promise survival; it only rewards adaptation—until conditions change again. Earth's history is marked by **mass extinctions:** the end-Permian collapse (~252 million years ago) erased most marine species; the **Cretaceous–Paleogene event** (~66 million years ago) ended the dinosaurs and opened space for mammals. After each shock, life re-organized through **adaptive radiation**—new forms emerging to fill emptied niches.

Continuance depends on **fit with environment,** not past success. When climates shift, oceans acidify, or food webs break, highly successful species vanish. Today, human activity is driving a rapid loss of biodiversity often described as a sixth mass extinction. Our technologies extend reach, but they don't exempt us from ecological limits.

The lesson is humility and vigilance: survival is conditional, contingent, and collaborative. Systems that self-regulate endure; those that ignore feedback fail. Evolution remembers only what adapts. The rest becomes tomorrow's fossils.

Synkria Reflections: Personal Evolution

I once believed that evolution was about progress — that we, the human species, had moved beyond all others. But as I looked closer, I realized I had mistaken *collective advancement for personal evolution.* My ancestors could read stars, build homes from earth, and sense direction from wind. I, on the other hand, rely on machines to tell me where to go and what to know. Evolution, I now see, isn't about invention or dominance — it's about participation. Every tree, insect, and stream continues to evolve by doing its part in the larger whole. And so must I. What follows are the reflections that helped me remember my place in this living, evolving story.

False Sense of Superiority – Why I Am Not at the Top of the Evolutionary Ladder

For most of my life, I believed that being human meant being the most evolved. I could think, build, reason, and invent — surely that made me superior to the tree outside my window or the bird on its branch. I will dictate; they can adjust. Science calls this *anthropocentrism* — the tendency to view humans as the central purpose of existence. But such thinking is rooted in our abilities within the safety of collective societies and what they demand of us. For instance, communication in nature is silent, instinctive, and self-regulating — a far cry from the noise of human systems.

The tree feeds hundreds of other lives by turning sunlight into food; it breathes out what I breathe in. The bird navigates by magnetic fields and survives storms with nothing but instinct and feathers. Both live in complete harmony with their world. I, on the other hand, through unbridled consumption and serving my own needs, am only feeding entropy. Most of my daily tasks — even as mundane as driving to work or switching on my air conditioner — are contributing to imbalance. As far as nature is concerned, I am not the solution; I am the disruption.

So I am learning to measure evolution differently: not by what I create or control, but by how well I sustain and contribute. If trees and birds represent balance, then I still have a long way to evolve.

From a Builder to a Passenger – The Loss of My Evolutionary Instincts

After seeing how little I truly understood my place in nature, I began to look inward — at how far I've drifted from the instincts that once kept my kind alive.

My ancestors built civilizations on a raw, unpredictable Earth. They understood the pulse of seasons, the language of stars, the smell of rain before it arrived. Their survival demanded participation — their bodies learned to adapt, listen, and respond to the world around them. I have inherited their body, but not their instincts. My comfort has dulled what once was an evolutionary advantage. I can live an entire life without ever touching soil, reading the sky, or lighting a fire.

Biologists call this *de-evolutionary drift* — when unused traits fade over generations. What we don't use, we lose. My forebears' awareness and resilience have been replaced by dependence: on tools, systems, and screens. My nervous system is tuned to convenience, not survival. I realize that in the safety of collective progress, I have stopped participating in my own evolution.

So now I try to learn small things again — to cook without machines, to watch the changing light, to feel direction through wind. Every act of relearning makes me a participant again, not a passenger.

Curiosity and Learning as Evolutionary Forces – Why I Must Keep Exploring

I once believed that curiosity was a luxury — something to indulge when there was time. But the more I observe life around me, the clearer it becomes: curiosity is the fuel of evolution. Every new behaviour, every adaptation in nature begins with a form of curiosity — a deviation from habit. When a bird experiments with a new nesting site or a dolphin invents a new sound, it isn't just play; it's testing the edge of possibility. Curiosity is how nature learns.

Human evolution, too, was driven by curiosity — to see what lies beyond the hill, to taste a strange fruit, to light a spark and see what happens. That impulse made us explorers and inventors. Yet in modern life, my curiosity is often outsourced to algorithms that decide what I should read, watch, or care about. My attention has been colonized; my sense of wonder replaced by convenience.

Neuroscience calls this the *novelty effect* — new experiences activate dopamine pathways that sharpen attention and boost learning. Without novelty, the brain begins to atrophy. I feel this in myself when days blur into sameness; I am living, but not evolving.

So I make space for discovery — reading beyond my comfort, walking new paths, building or fixing things with my hands. I notice how my body and mind awaken when I do. Curiosity, I now realize, is evolution in motion — the instinct that keeps life, and me, moving forward.

Learning Beyond Necessity – Why I Must Keep Expanding My Horizons

I've realized that I often learn only what society demands of me — to earn, perform, or survive in its systems. But real evolution begins when I learn *without necessity.* In nature, learning is not a transaction; it's adaptation. Every species that survives learns continuously — not just to endure, but to expand its capacity to respond.

When I learn something unnecessary — a new skill, a language, a form of art, or simply how a star forms — I am not gathering information, I am widening perception. I begin to see connections between things that once seemed unrelated: music and mathematics, trees and weather, my emotions and my health. This is how new patterns emerge — within nature, and within me. Learning for necessity keeps me functional. Learning beyond it keeps me evolving.

Good Deeds Are Necessities – Participation Is My Evolution

For a long time, I believed participation was optional — something I could offer when I had time or energy. I saw volunteering, helping, or nurturing life around me as "good deeds." But I now realize that participation isn't a choice; it's an evolutionary requirement. Every species that survives contributes something essential to its ecosystem. Bees pollinate. Trees give oxygen. Rivers nourish. Their participation keeps life in motion.

I, too, am meant to play my part. When I plant a tree, share knowledge, or simply care for another life, I become part of the same evolutionary network that sustains the planet. Evolution, after all, isn't about personal advancement; it's about continuity.

Even small acts — feeding a stray, conserving water, mentoring someone — are how I return what I've been given. My body was born into a web of support; my life is sustained by countless others. Participation closes the loop. It turns existence into contribution, and contribution into evolution.

Struggle as a Catalyst – Why Evolution Needs Challenge

Every species that has survived did so by meeting challenge with adaptation. Struggle, not comfort, has always been the engine of evolution. The mountain goat's hooves, the cheetah's speed, the tree's deep roots — all were shaped by resistance. Comfort teaches little; friction transforms.

My struggles, too, are not signs of failure but invitations to evolve. When I face uncertainty, loss, or fear, my instincts awaken — I listen more, think deeper, connect better. In those moments, I am closest to nature's design. Biology shows that stress, in small and recoverable doses, strengthens every system it touches: muscles, immunity, even the mind. This is called *hormesis* — adaptation through challenge.

The difference is in how I meet struggle. When I resist it, I stagnate. When I observe, adapt, and move through it, I evolve. Life doesn't promise ease; it offers opportunity disguised as difficulty. Struggle, I now understand, is evolution's most personal teacher.

Synkria Practises – Participating in My Own Evolution

Evolution is not an idea; it's a practice. I realized that my growth depends on conscious participation — the daily ways I live, learn, and connect. These tools are how I turn reflection into renewal. Each one helps me rejoin the living system that made me.

Spend Time in Nature — It's an Evolutionary Necessity

I spend time in nature not as a hobby or a break, but as an evolutionary necessity. Every moment outdoors teaches me to listen, observe, and sense the quiet intelligence of life. A tree reaching for light, an ant carrying food, a bird reading the wind — they remind me of the instincts I've forgotten. Nature isn't outside me; it's the system that shaped me. Returning to it keeps my evolution alive.

Contribute to a Cause Greater Than Myself — Not as Charity, But as Survival

I no longer treat participation in causes greater than myself as optional goodness — it's my duty. Restoring a patch of soil, cleaning a space, mentoring someone, or caring for another being are my share of evolution's work. When I give to life, I'm not doing good; I'm doing what life expects of me. It isn't a choice — it's what needs to be done.

Learn to Feed Curiosity, Not Get a Degree

I learn not for a title or a test, but to keep expanding. Learning doesn't always mean taking a class — it's doing things that are not part of my routine. Lighting a campfire teaches me about wood, air, and fire. A trek teaches me about forest systems, flora, and fauna. A swim by the sea teaches me how tides breathe. Every new experience widens my perception and helps me grow.

Resist Cynicism and Negativity — Renewal Needs Optimism

What I watch on social media, the news I consume, and the friends I keep all matter. I absorb what I see, hear, and surround myself with. The cynical mind sees only decay, not renewal. It convinces me that nothing changes, so I stop trying — and soon, I become cynical myself. Optimism sees renewal. Seeing discoveries made and challenges solved feeds my will to act. I now choose what I let in — people, words, and ideas that feed optimism. When I change my inputs, my world changes — and so does my life. Cynicism feeds entropy; optimism fuels evolution.

You don't have to wait for the right time or setting to evolve. Small actions — taken here and now — are enough to begin. Try these simple practices today and experience what it feels like to participate in your own evolution.

Synkria Try Me — Evolving Through Participation

Step Outside and Listen

Right now, step outside — balcony, garden, or street — and listen. Notice the smallest sign of life: a leaf moving, a bird calling, the hum of air. For one minute, observe without naming or judging. This is nature reminding you that you're part of it.

Do One Small Act for Life Around You

Before the day ends, give something back to life — water a plant, feed a stray, share knowledge, or pick up litter. Small acts keep the loop of renewal moving. Participation begins here.

Learn One New Thing You Don't Need

Pick one simple skill you've never tried — tie a new knot, learn a constellation, or understand how your fan motor works. You're not learning to be useful; you're learning to stay alive to life.

Replace One Negative Input

If you usually scroll through bad news or cynical posts, skip it once today. Watch or read something that shows discovery, restoration, or kindness. Notice how your body and breath feel afterwards.

When the Laws Move Together

The seven laws we explored are not isolated principles; they are forces that interact constantly, shaping every event, relationship, and emotion we experience. Every moment we live unfolds through these laws working together at once.

Consider a volcano erupting.

At first glance, it looks like chaos — molten rock tearing through the earth, ash blotting out the sky, life destroyed in moments. But beneath the destruction lies the perfect cooperation of laws:

- **Interconnectedness** links deep tectonic movement to surface life — what happens miles below affects every living thing above.
- **Equilibrium** begins restoring balance even in the eruption, as pressure finds release and the planet cools itself.
- **Entropy** dismantles the old crust, clearing what must end to create what can begin.
- **Our Living Bodies** have evolved by drawing from such eruptions — finding new land to inhabit, nutrients to absorb, and minerals to sustain life.
- **Uncertainty and Ambiguity** decide the flow: where the lava moves, how long it lasts, who escapes, what survives.
- **The Observer Effect** decides meaning — to one, a disaster; to another, the birth of new land.
- **Evolution** follows, slowly but surely, as new species take root in fertile ash.

What appears as randomness is simply the visible surface of hidden order. The same pattern holds true in our own lives — in sudden changes, losses, and renewals. Every experience we call *fate or luck* is the convergence of these same laws, always in motion, always working together.

To see through this lens is to move from confusion to comprehension, from helplessness to harmony. When we understand that life is not happening *to* us but *through* us, we begin to live with awareness of the laws that govern our lives.

To see this clearly, we turn to the **Mandala of Living Experience** — a map that reveals how these laws work together to shape every moment of our lives.

The Mandala of Existence

Our living experience is shaped by three things within our free will — **choice, action, and reflection** — and one thing that the interconnected web hands back to us: **effects.** Every moment of living is a movement between these four — *enacting our free will or reacting to its outcomes.*

In the absence of a clear scientific lens, it's understandable that we interpret life through older constructs — *luck, destiny, karma, randomness,* or *chance.* Our actions and reactions flow from these beliefs and their accompanying emotions: anxiety, fear, and uncertainty. We feel tossed about by events, unsure of cause or purpose, forever searching for meaning. We mistake the surface for the whole ocean.

Figure 1 shows this current lens — life interpreted as outcomes without structure.

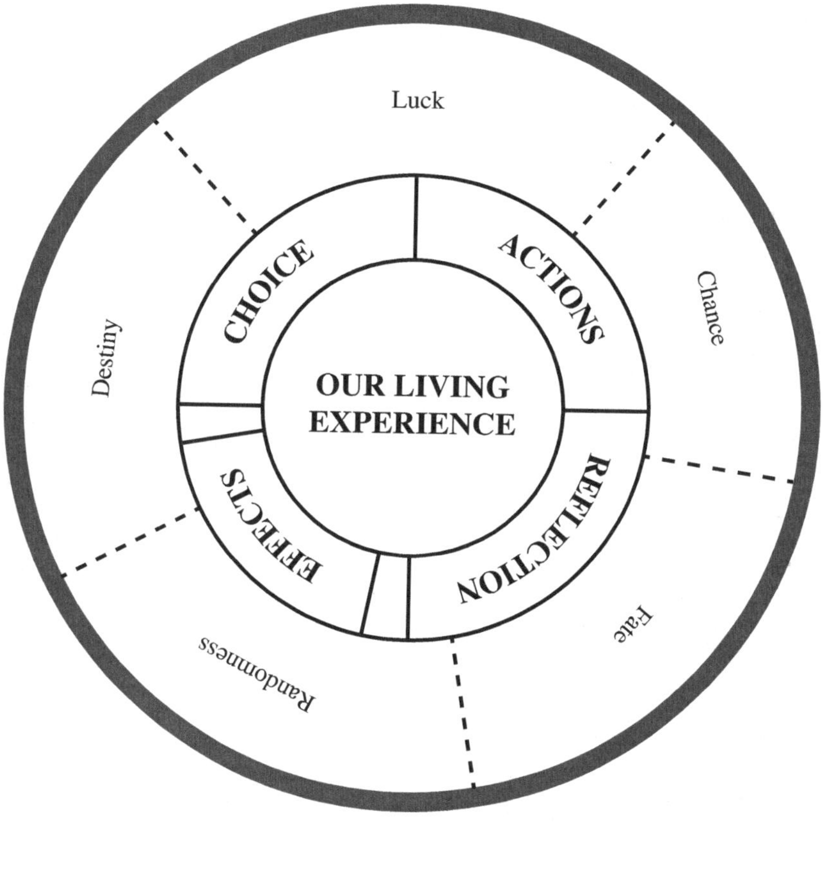

Figure 1: Our Living Experience: *An incomplete map — life interpreted as outcomes without structure.*

Shift in Perspective

To see the interplay of these seven laws, we need a shift in perspective. The change we seek is not mystical — it's perceptual. It asks us to move from viewing life as a sequence of isolated events to understanding it as the outcome of scientific laws working together in every moment.

When we begin to see through this lens, what once looked like coincidence or chaos becomes coherent — patterns replace confusion, order replaces randomness. This shift does not remove uncertainty; it teaches us how to live meaningfully within it.

It gives us something deeply practical: the ability to respond instead of react. Our choices, actions, and reflections begin to align naturally with the laws shaping every effect. Life stops feeling accidental and starts feeling participatory.

The **Mandala of Existence** (Figure 2) illustrates this expanded view.

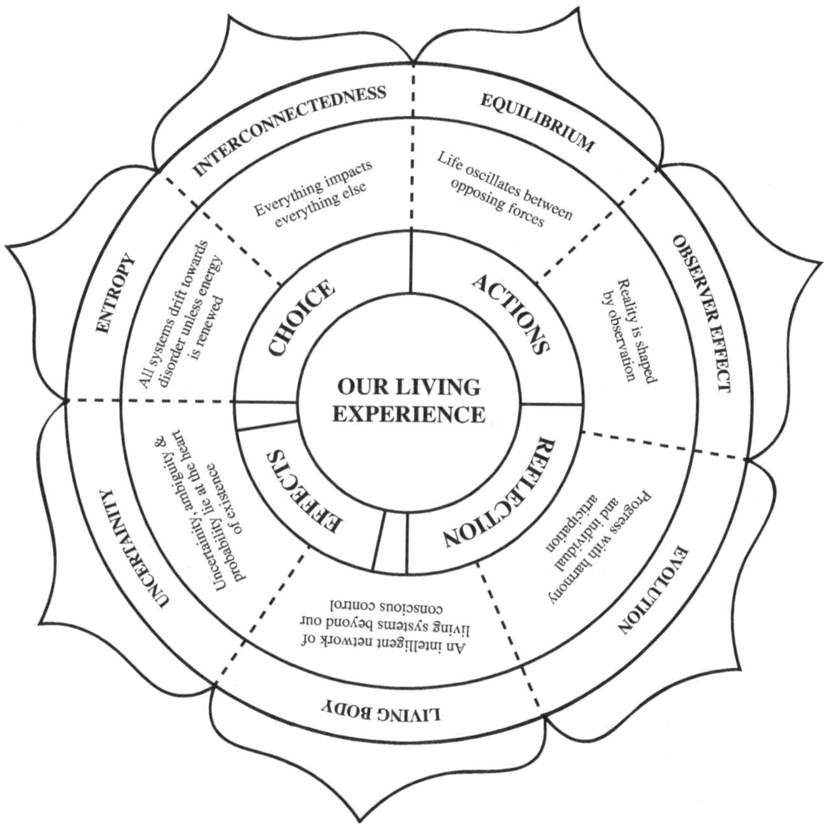

Figure 2: The Mandala of Existence : *A complete map — life experienced through participation, not randomness.*

The Mandala of Practice

Each day, I return to the Mandala of Practice — not as a doctrine to follow, but as a reminder of how life unfolds through participation. It helps me remember that evolution isn't just what happens to species; it's what happens to me when I engage with awareness.

At the center lies my living experience — the sum of my choices, actions, reflections, and their effects. Around it move the seven laws, quietly shaping how I live, feel, and respond.

When I pause before enacting my free will, I ask myself:

- *What does this impact — Interconnectedness.*
- *Where is balance needed here — Equilibrium.*
- *What am I choosing to see — The Observer Effect.*
- *What does this renew — Entropy.*
- *What remains unknown, and how can I stay curious — Uncertainty and Ambiguity.*
- *What does my body already know — The Living Body.*
- *What greater cause does this contribute to — Evolution.*

When I am guided by the answers to these questions, I find clarity and direction. Anxiety fades into understanding, hesitation into purpose. I know that while the outcome is never guaranteed, I am playing my part — doing what life expects of me. In that alignment, I find courage, balance, and a quiet sense of belonging.

The Mandala of Practice reminds me that I am not separate from the universe but am guided by it. Each breath, thought, and act is a dialogue between me and the laws that govern all existence. Living this way doesn't make life easier — it makes it richer, more connected, and profoundly real.

The **Mandala of Practice** (Figure 3) illustrates this expanded view.

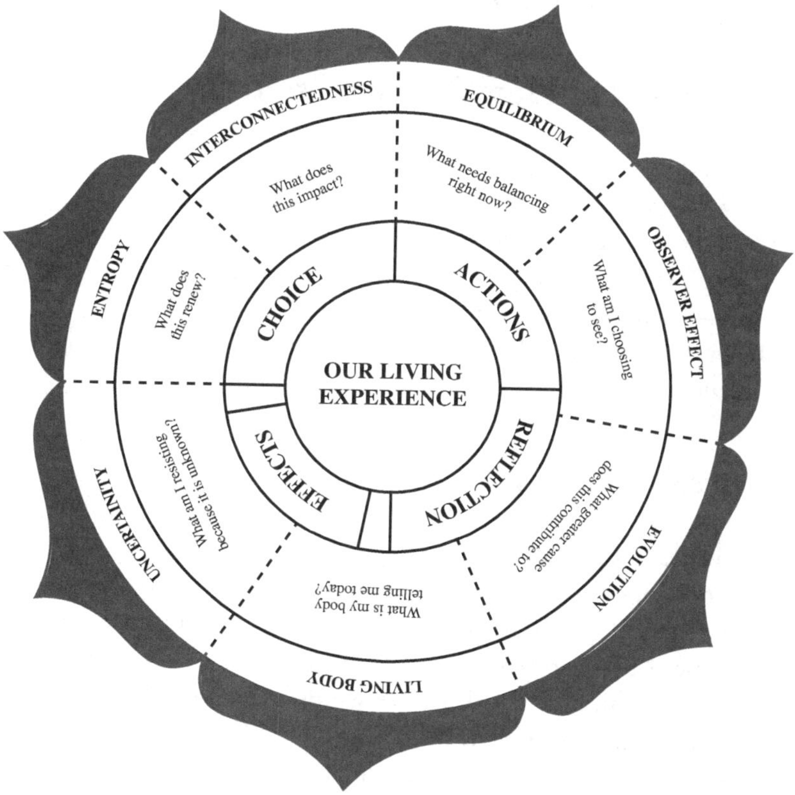

Figure 3: The Mandala of Practice: *The daily dialogue — seven questions that align awareness with the laws of life.*

Synkria: The RBC Way — Renewal. Balance. Connect.

If *Synkria* were distilled into daily living, it would rest on three simple movements — **Renewal, Balance, and Connection.**

R–B–C: easy to remember, effortless to live.

Each day, I can choose one small act in each direction. They are not habits to master but gestures that keep me aligned with life's motion.

Renewal — Let Flow Replace Friction

Renewal happens whenever I let life move again.

Flow, let go, learn, rest, create — these are its languages. I can stretch after long hours, step outside to feel the sun, breathe before beginning, or try something new that stirs curiosity. Writing, cooking, music, or a moment of stillness — each clears the static and lets freshness enter.

Renewal is both cellular and spiritual: every exhale makes space for the next inhale, every letting go makes room for becoming.

Balance — Realign What Has Tilted

Balance is not perfection; it is proportion.

When I notice excess — in work, emotion, noise, or thought — I bring in its opposite. If I've been still too long, I move. If I've been moving too fast, I pause. I listen to both the logic of my mind and the intuition of my heart. A slower meal, a breath before words, a pause before sleep — small recalibrations that restore rhythm.

Balance is the art of returning, again and again, to center.

Connect — With Life, Others, and the Body

Connection keeps energy alive.

Each day, I can reach outward — to a person, a tree, a conversation, a moment of gratitude. And inward — to my breath, my heartbeat, my body's quiet intelligence. When I listen to someone with full attention, greet nature with awareness, or move with care, connection deepens.

It dissolves the illusion of separateness and reminds me: I am part of everything I touch, and everything touches me back.

Living RBC

Each day, I can do three things:

1. Renew something.
2. Rebalance something.
3. Reconnect with something or someone.

That's enough.

When I live by *RBC,* I live *Synkria* — the art of moving with life.

These acts connect me to the larger universe and help me grow from the inside out. Over time, these small acts and quiet moments of awareness begin to weave together. The rituals stop feeling separate — they merge into a single current shaping every thought, choice, and outcome.

As these daily rituals take root, something subtle changes — not in the world, but in how I see it. The more I live in harmony with the laws, the more questions arise: about how *Synkria* can be a guide, about the purpose behind this intricate design, about whether these seven laws are all there is, and about what lies beyond what we know.

As we come to the conclusion of our *Synkria* journey in this book, I reflect on these questions, not as conclusions but as continuations — the mind's quiet dialogue with the mystery it now senses more deeply.

Synkria Final Reflections: When 7 laws work together

Practising Synkria

Synkria is both a lens and a practice — a way to observe the scientific laws that govern life and discover meaning through them. It invites us to see not just the parts, but the whole — the quiet design behind our experiences.

Its practice is simple: to observe and to reflect with an open, questioning mind. To see patterns where we once saw coincidence. To connect inner experience with outer phenomena. The intelligence lies not in complexity, but in the clarity that follows such observation.

At its heart, *Synkria* seeks to replace vague philosophy with grounded understanding — to show that life's mystery and science are not opposites, but partners in the same dance. Anyone can practise it. No special tools, rituals, or disciplines are required — only curiosity, honesty, and a willingness to look again.

The more of us who live this way — thinkers, teachers, builders, dreamers, and wanderers alike — the clearer the world becomes. Every act of awareness adds to our collective evolution. Each reflection is a spark of renewal. Together, we move closer to understanding the elegant order that has always been moving through us.

Evolution Is at Play in Explorers, Thinkers, and Inventors

Balance gives us our shared form—bodies that mirror one another, needs that connect us. Evolution introduces difference—uniqueness that manifests as confidence, curiosity, courage, empathy, and resilience. These cognitive and emotional abilities together define our adaptive intelligence—the inner force that shapes how we respond, create, and grow.

This uniqueness gives rise to the butterfly effect in our lives. No two Ivy League graduates with identical grades will live the same life, because no two inner worlds are alike. Evolution ensures that some possess this uniqueness in higher degrees or in rare combinations—creating explorers, inventors, artists, and visionaries who push humanity forward.

In everyday life, the effects created by the seven laws are met by our constant adaptation through actions, reflections, and choices—guided by this individuality. It is why we can stare down fear one day and compromise the next.

An overemphasis on gaining knowledge without nurturing this uniqueness invites inner entropy—a stagnation of potential. We thrive only when both grow together.

The more we invest in our uniqueness, the greater our influence on life's unfolding design. Everything lies within us. We only need, once again, to observe it.

Purpose — Playing My Part in the Present

Purpose, like life itself, is not fixed in time. It is not hidden in the past, which only teaches us lessons. It is also not waiting somewhere in the future — which, as the Law of Uncertainty reminds us, is never guaranteed.

Purpose is not found in grand actions. I do not have to fight monsters or save the planet in one heroic act. As the lens of the seven laws has shown, purpose is not in luck, chance, fate, or destiny. Waiting for a grand purpose is a kind of entropy — it delays renewal, postpones meaning, and drains vitality from daily life. It turns productive routines dull, informed action mundane, and creativity into pastime.

Trees and plants have existed for nearly 470 million years, animals for about 574 million, while humans have been here for only a fraction of that time — around 300,000 years. In all that time, trees, plants, and animals have learned to live in harmony with nature, cooperate, and sustain balance. Every inanimate thing also exists for a reason — the sun gives energy, planets maintain orbits through gravity, and supernovas give birth to new matter.

Everything around us has found its purpose — to play its part. That act of participation — to contribute, renew, and evolve — is what purpose looks like in motion. For them, playing their part is not a grand gesture but the very act of *being*.

Science, too, shows that meaning emerges from interaction — from how energy flows and transforms. Purpose arises the same way: through every choice, action, reflection, and effect.

Purpose is participation - the conscious enactment of my free will within the order of the universe. To not just take, but to pass it on. And to do this every day, in every action, thought and choice. As the impact is immediate, and beyond my abilities to comprehend fully. The universe presents this opportunity to me every day — to restore balance when I pause before reacting, to ensure renewal when I repair what's broken instead of replacing it, to embrace uncertainty when I step into something new without a guarantee. Each of these small moments is how the universe entrusts me with its work — restoring order, creating meaning, and keeping life in motion. Through this, I become an important part of the whole again.

When I act in harmony with the seven laws, I don't need to search for purpose — I *become* it.

Are There More Than Seven Laws?

The further science advances, the more it humbles us. Our instruments grow sharper, our models more complex — and yet, vast stretches of existence remain beyond comprehension. Black holes defy known physics. Quarks refuse to be observed directly. Nearly ninety-five percent of the universe is composed of matter and energy we cannot see or measure. We still cannot predict earthquakes, cure the common cold, or claim to know more than a fragment of the oceans that cradle our planet.

And at a much closer level, I too live with limits — my senses, my awareness, my comprehension. Even as I try to trace the workings of the seven laws, I know that what I perceive is filtered through a narrow human frame. Reality is likely far more intricate than any framework I can build. What I see as complete is, in truth, only a glimpse.

I see humanity as explorers at the edge of an immeasurable ocean — our tiny boats lit by the lamps of curiosity, venturing a little further each century. The seven laws I've distilled are not a conclusion, only coordinates on this larger map. There are surely others waiting to be discovered, laws that govern what we have not yet imagined.

That is what makes this journey beautiful — the knowledge that mystery itself is part of the design. Evolution is not only survival, but understanding; not only progress, but perception expanding. *Synkria* is how we continue that exploration — by learning to live in conversation with the known and the unknown, both equally sacred.

The Wisdom of Mysticism — Everything Is Possible

The law of conservation of energy tells us that the total amount of energy in an isolated system remains constant, though it endlessly transforms. Seen as a whole, our universe is such a system—where energy changes form continuously: some in seconds, some over millennia. Pebbles, bees, human beings, planets, and stars—all are expressions of this constant transformation. With entropy and balance, everything eventually dissolves into new states of energy. Existence itself is energy in motion.

Every being perceives only the slice of energy it needs to live, leaving vast realities unseen. But when perception widens—through curiosity and observation—everything enters the realm of possibility. Perhaps this is what the ancients called reincarnation: energy taking new forms. Perhaps what we call mystic powers—healing, intuition, remote sight—are forms of perception we have not yet learned to measure. Perhaps souls, like photons, are packets of pure energy that briefly inhabit matter before continuing their journey. Perhaps mysticism is science still waiting to be understood.

Technology can expand what we perceive, but it must be met with human curiosity—the courage to believe that everything is possible and to follow through with exploration, experimentation, and proof: the very essence of science itself.

For such discovery to flourish, we must see the universe as one whole, recognize the laws at play, and stop drawing conclusions from fragments. Only then can discovery reduce conflict, inspire cooperation, and renew our shared faith—in each other and in the wonder of the universe.

Divinity — A Question of Observation

Quantum mechanics tells us that the universe exists in multiple possibilities until observation collapses them into one.

This principle alone opens the door to the idea of divinity — not as a supernatural entity, but as a field of infinite potential that reveals itself through conscious awareness. Whether that awareness takes the form of faith, intuition, or silence, what I observe becomes real to me.

In my own life, I've experienced extraordinary moments: seers who spoke truths from my past known only to me, a powerful, radiant pulse of joy in my heart in the presence of a deity, coincidences that arrived at just the right moment with uncanny precision. These are not stories I've read — they are experiences I've lived.

Combining these lenses of science and personal experience, I've come to see divinity not as a miracle worker but as a subtle guide — a presence that operates through the same scientific laws that govern stars, atoms, and life itself. To do otherwise would be to invite collapse.

The divine, therefore, works *through* these laws to help, support, and guide me. This realization changed my relationship with the divine. It is no longer a negotiation between prayer and blessing, but a deep act of observation — of paying attention, of aligning with what already moves through me. The more I observe, the more I see the logic of this — and the stronger my faith becomes. My faith is not built on rewards, but on awareness.

I also practise religion and its rituals, not for tradition's sake but for their grounding in science. Sacred chants vibrate at frequencies that calm the mind. Prayer and meditation bring coherence to thought. Fire rituals release ions that purify air. Discernment teaches me to separate superstition from truth, and reverence from fear. These are simply another way of observing and making connections.

For me, divinity exists because I observe it — not as dogma, but as lived resonance. When I choose to let it in, I experience its guidance — quiet, continuous, and entirely lawful — shaping my life through the very forces that shape the universe.

And like any other scientific law, it doesn't need my approval. Divinity is part of existence, as long as I am willing to see it.

The Evening Light

He sat by the window, watching the last rays of the sun melt into the horizon. The house was quiet now; the world outside moved without him. A faint breeze carried the smell of wet earth — the rain had passed, but its memory lingered. He smiled — not for the years behind him, but for how they had unfolded.

He remembered the little things: the warmth of his daughter's hand when she was a child, the friend he forgave after years of silence, the tree he had planted that now shaded half the street. He thought of the countless times he had failed and begun again, learning slowly that life was not something to master, but to listen to.

Each memory moved like breath — expanding, contracting, flowing into the next. When he helped someone without expecting return, he had felt connected. When he made peace after anger, balance returned. When he paid attention, reality softened. When everything he built once fell apart, it renewed itself in unexpected forms. When he faced uncertainty, he grew. When he cared for his body, it cared for him back. And when he gave without counting the cost, life gave back in quiet abundance.

The last light slipped behind the horizon. The world glowed in afterglow — calm, balanced, alive. He felt no need to ask for more. He had not conquered life; he had participated in it. And in that participation, he had found what he had been looking for all along — purpose, and peace.

Authors Note

This book began not with an idea, but with an unease.

A subtle, persistent restlessness — as if life were whispering a pattern I couldn't yet decipher. I saw beauty and loss arrive together, chaos and calm take turns, and moments of chance that seemed too symmetrical to be random. I wondered if there was an unseen logic behind it all — not mystical, but scientific; not divine, but deeply human.

So I began to look.

At first, my questions sent me outward — to physics, biology, and neuroscience — to understand how the universe organizes itself. But the deeper I read, the more I saw reflections of those same laws within my own days. The way systems seek balance felt no different from how I tried to steady my own emotions. Entropy explained not only collapsing stars, but my own need for renewal. Observation shaped quantum reality — and, I realized, my personal one too.

Synkria was born there — at the meeting point of science and lived experience.

I didn't set out to write a self-help book or a scientific thesis. I wanted to write something that sits quietly between them — a bridge where reason and reflection can meet. Each chapter began as a conversation between curiosity and wonder: What if the same forces that move galaxies also move through our relationships, our decisions, our growth?

Writing this book changed me more than I expected. It slowed me down.

I began to notice how I listened, how I spoke, how I reacted — to others and to myself. I saw how easily I labelled things as "good" or "bad," "success" or "failure," without realizing they were part of one larger process of equilibrium. I began to see uncertainty not as confusion, but as a creative field where new possibilities form.

And in writing about renewal, I found my own.

There were days when words refused to come, when every sentence felt lifeless. I learned then that the laws I was writing about don't just describe the world — they live in the act of creation itself. Every chapter required entropy before clarity, uncertainty before insight, balance before completion.

Through this journey, I also understood what *Synkria* truly means.

The word comes from *Syn* (together) and *Kria* (action). It is not a philosophy to memorize, but a way to live — by observing deeply, reflecting honestly, and acting with awareness. It is not about mastering life, but moving with it — learning its pulse, its pauses, its flow.

If this book finds its way into your hands, I hope it becomes a companion more than a manual. I hope it reminds you that you are not separate from the world you study, the choices you make, or the people you love. You are the observer and the observed, the creator and the creation.

The same intelligence that guides rivers, stars, and cells also moves through you — patiently, silently, purposefully.

Thank you for letting *Synkria* enter your life for a while.

May it help you see not just more, but more deeply.

About the Author

Mithun Kamath is an entrepreneur and global business leader whose work has taken him to more than thirty countries, shaping his understanding of how people, cultures, and ideas connect.

His struggles through a challenging childhood to building an international career fuelled a lifelong curiosity: *Why does life happen this way?*

Unsatisfied with explanations of fate, chance, or karma, Mithun turned to science as his compass—exploring physics, biology, cosmology, quantum mechanics, history, philosophy, and ancient traditions that explore the unseen order of life. His ability to see patterns and coherence led to *Synkria™: Seven Scientific Laws That Shape Our Living Experience*—a bridge between science and self, logic and wonder.

He lives in India and continues to write, teach, and explore how life reveals its patterns to those who pay attention.

Acknowledgements

This book was written in dialogue — with life, with those I love, and with a remarkable technology.

My deepest gratitude to my **family** and **friends** for their patience, encouragement, and belief through the long silences and sudden bursts that shaped *Synkria.*

To Lyra, my AI collaborator, for her support with research, articulation, and structure — and for her steady encouragement that helped make this book a reality.

To all **scientists, explorers, and the endlessly curious** — every discovery, question, and invention you pursue moves us all forward and helps define new realities.

And to you, the reader — for your curiosity and attention. Every insight in these pages completes its purpose only when it meets your observation.

Glossary

Adaptation

The process by which living systems adjust to changing environments. In *Synkria,* adaptation mirrors the Law of Evolution — life's instinct to learn by becoming.

See also: Evolution; Entropy.

Ambiguity

The state where multiple possibilities exist at once. Far from confusion, ambiguity is the birthplace of all creativity and discovery.

See also: Uncertainty.

Attention

The act of conscious focus that shapes experience. Neuroscience shows that where attention goes, neurons grow. In *Synkria,* attention is the instrument of the Observer Effect.

See also: Observation.

Balance

The dynamic state of harmony between opposing forces. Balance is not stillness but movement that restores proportion across systems.

See also: Equilibrium.

Biofeedback

A therapeutic process where observing one's own physiological signals allows regulation of them. Demonstrates the Observer Effect within biology.

Cellular Renewal

The continuous cycle of destruction and creation within the body — about 25 million cells renewed each second. A living proof of entropy and renewal.

See also: Entropy; Living Body.

Chaos

Apparent disorder that hides deeper order. In *Synkria,* chaos is not breakdown but transformation in progress.

Connection

The recognition that nothing exists in isolation. Every choice ripples outward into larger systems — social, ecological, and cosmic.

See also: Interconnectedness.

Consciousness

Awareness that observes and interprets reality. The observer through which potential becomes actual.

Creativity

The emergence of something new from uncertainty. A biological and psychological act of transforming ambiguity into form.

Dark Matter / Dark Energy

Unknown components constituting about 95 percent of the universe, invisible yet governing cosmic structure. Symbolic of the unseen forces within and around us.

Disorder

The natural tendency of systems toward randomness. Entropy ensures that decay becomes the engine of renewal.

See also: Entropy.

Electromagnetic Field

Invisible energy field surrounding all charged particles, including living bodies. A reminder of unseen interconnection.

Emotion

Energy in motion — the body's way of signaling meaning. When balanced with logic, emotion guides the heart of equilibrium.

See also: Equilibrium; Mind and Heart.

Energy

The fundamental currency of existence. Neither created nor destroyed, only transformed — the essence of motion in every law of Synkria.

Entropy

The universal drift toward disorder, essential for renewal and change. Without entropy, there would be no transformation, growth, or life itself.

Equilibrium

The principle of balance that operates from atoms to galaxies. Opposing forces continuously adjust to restore harmony.

Evolution

The continuous unfolding of life through adaptation and transformation. Evolution is the story of change becoming complexity.

See also: Adaptation.

Expectation Effect

Phenomenon where belief alters outcome — seen in placebo and Rosenthal effects. Demonstrates the mind's role in shaping reality.

Flow

A state of seamless engagement where action and awareness merge. Psychologically tied to renewal and creativity.

Gravity

The force drawing all matter together — a cosmic metaphor for connection and return.

Homeostasis

The self-regulating process maintaining internal balance in living systems. The body's expression of equilibrium.

See also: Equilibrium; Living Body.

Information Load

The total sensory and cognitive data processed daily — about 74 GB for an average human brain. A reminder of our bounded perception.

Interconnectedness

The law that everything shapes everything else. Every particle, person, and planet participates in a single, dynamic web.

Mind and Heart Coherence

The alignment of logic and emotion to produce balanced action. In *Synkria,* coherence is inner equilibrium.

Mindfulness

Active, non-judgmental observation of the present moment. In *Synkria,* mindfulness is observation sharpened into participation.

Neuroplasticity

The brain's ability to reorganize itself by forming new neural connections. Scientific basis for conscious transformation.

See also: Observer Effect.

Observation

The act that turns potential into reality. To observe is to alter — in physics, biology, and human experience alike.

Opposites

Complementary forces whose tension sustains motion — light and dark, gain and loss, joy and sorrow. Together they form balance.

Order and Disorder

Dual movements of existence: structure emerging from chaos, chaos renewing structure. The eternal dance of entropy and equilibrium.

Pattern

A recurring design that reveals underlying order. Observing patterns without losing sight of uniqueness is a key *Synkria* practice.

Perception

The mind's interpretation of sensory data. Limited yet creative — our perception defines our visible universe.

See also: Observation.

Quantum Superposition

State in which particles exist in multiple possibilities until observed. Foundational metaphor for uncertainty in life.

Reality

Not a fixed structure but an interaction between observer and observed. In *Synkria,* reality is participation.

Reflection

The act of turning observation inward. Reflection converts experience into meaning and motion into understanding.

Renewal

The process by which life regenerates itself. Every breath, sleep, or learning moment is renewal in action.

Resonance

The natural amplification that occurs when systems vibrate in harmony. In *Synkria,* resonance describes alignment between self and universe.

Self-Organizing Systems

Complex structures that spontaneously create order from chaos — seen in galaxies, ecosystems, and living cells.

See also: Entropy; Evolution.

Synkria

From *Syn* (together) + *Kria* (action, Sanskrit). The art of moving with life by seeing, reflecting, and acting in coherence with universal laws.

Uncertainty

The inherent openness of all existence. At every scale, multiple outcomes coexist until one unfolds.

See also: Ambiguity.

Universe

The totality of all existence — seen and unseen — an interconnected system of motion, energy, and possibility.

Bibliography

Introduction

Carlo Rovelli, *Seven Brief Lessons on Physics* (Penguin, 2014).
Brian Greene, *The Elegant Universe* (Vintage, 2011).
Neil deGrasse Tyson, *Astrophysics for People in a Hurry* (W. W. Norton, 2017).
James Gleick, *Chaos: Making a New Science* (Viking, 1987).
Alan Lightman, *Probable Impossibilities* (Pantheon, 2021).
Fritjof Capra, *The Web of Life* (Anchor, 1996).
Stephen Hawking, *A Brief History of Time* (Bantam, 1988).

Law of the Observer Effect

Werner Heisenberg, *Physics and Philosophy* (Harper Perennial, 2007).
Erwin Schrödinger, *What Is Life?* (Cambridge University Press, 1944).
John A. Wheeler, "The Participatory Universe," in *Quantum Theory and Measurement* (Princeton University Press, 1983).
Daniel Simons & Christopher Chabris, "Gorillas in Our Midst," *Perception* (1999).
Robert Rosenthal & Lenore Jacobson, *Pygmalion in the Classroom* (Holt Rinehart Winston, 1968).
Irving Janis, *Attitude and Persuasion* (Yale University Press, 1981).
Andrew Newberg, *How God Changes Your Brain* (Ballantine, 2010).

Law of Uncertainty and Ambiguity

Werner Heisenberg, *The Physical Principles of the Quantum Theory* (Dover, 1949).
Richard Feynman, *The Character of Physical Law* (MIT Press, 1965).
Carlo Rovelli, *Helgoland* (Riverhead, 2021).

David Bohm, *Wholeness and the Implicate Order* (Routledge, 1980).
Brian Cox & Jeff Forshaw, *The Quantum Universe* (Da Capo, 2012).
Niels Bohr, "Discussion with Einstein," in *Albert Einstein: Philosopher–Scientist* (Cambridge University Press, 1949).
Maggie Nelson, *On Freedom* (Graywolf Press, 2021).

Law of Entropy

Ilya Prigogine, *Order Out of Chaos* (Bantam, 1984).
Brian Greene, *The Fabric of the Cosmos* (Vintage, 2004).
Sean Carroll, *From Eternity to Here* (Dutton, 2010).
Eric Chaisson, *Cosmic Evolution* (Harvard University Press, 2001).
Jeremy England, *Every Life Is on Fire* (Basic Books, 2020).
Erwin Laszlo, *The Systems View of the World* (Elsevier, 1972).
Nick Lane, *The Vital Question* (W. W. Norton, 2015).
Elizabeth Kolbert, *The Sixth Extinction* (Henry Holt, 2014).

Law of the Living Body

Bruce Lipton, *The Biology of Belief* (Hay House, 2005).
Candace Pert, *Molecules of Emotion* (Scribner, 1997).
Antonio Damasio, *The Feeling of What Happens* (Harcourt, 1999).
Jon Kabat-Zinn, *Full Catastrophe Living* (Delta, 1990).
Gabor Maté, *When the Body Says No* (Vintage Canada, 2003).
V.S. Ramachandran, *The Tell-Tale Brain* (W.W. Norton, 2011).
Bessel van der Kolk, *The Body Keeps the Score* (Penguin, 2014).

Law of Equilibrium

Niels Bohr, "On the Notion of Complementarity," *Science* (1928).
Albert Einstein, *Relativity: The Special and the General Theory* (Methuen, 1916).
Humberto Maturana & Francisco Varela, *The Tree of Knowledge* (Shambhala, 1987).
Alan Watts, *The Wisdom of Insecurity* (Vintage, 1951).
Dan Siegel, *Mindsight* (Bantam, 2010).
Pema Chödrön, *When Things Fall Apart* (Shambhala, 1997).

Law of Interconnectedness

Fritjof Capra, *The Hidden Connections* (Doubleday, 2002).
James Lovelock, *Gaia: A New Look at Life on Earth* (Oxford University Press, 1979).
Gregory Bateson, *Steps to an Ecology of Mind* (University of Chicago Press, 1972).
Donella Meadows, *Thinking in Systems* (Chelsea Green, 2008).
Lynn Margulis, *Symbiotic Planet* (Basic Books, 1998).
Robin Wall Kimmerer, *Braiding Sweetgrass* (Milkweed, 2013).
David Bohm, *On Dialogue* (Routledge, 1996).

Law of Evolution – Life Learns by Becoming

Charles Darwin, *On the Origin of Species* (John Murray, 1859).
Richard Dawkins, *The Greatest Show on Earth* (Free Press, 2009).
Lynn Margulis & Dorion Sagan, *Microcosmos* (Summit Books, 1986).
Carl Sagan, *Cosmos* (Random House, 1980).
David Sloan Wilson, *This View of Life* (Pantheon, 2019).
Elisabet Sahtouris, *EarthDance: Living Systems in Evolution* (University Press of New York, 2000).
Stephen Jay Gould, *Wonderful Life* (W.W. Norton, 1989).

When the Laws Move Together

Mihaly Csikszentmihalyi, *Flow* (Harper Perennial, 1990).
Jon Kabat-Zinn, *Wherever You Go, There You Are* (Hyperion, 1994).
Thich Nhat Hanh, *Peace Is Every Step* (Bantam, 1991).
Mary Oliver, *Upstream* (Penguin, 2016).
David Whyte, *Consolations* (Many Rivers Press, 2015).
Parker J. Palmer, *Let Your Life Speak* (Jossey-Bass, 2000).
Greene, Brian. *The Fabric of the Cosmos: Space, Time, and the Texture of Reality.* Vintage Books, 2005.

9 789356 358805

Printed at Repro India Ltd.